LIFELINES

Michelangelo Merisi da Caravaggio

Karin Hellwig

PRESTEL

MUNICH · BERLIN · LONDON · NEW YORK

CONTENTS

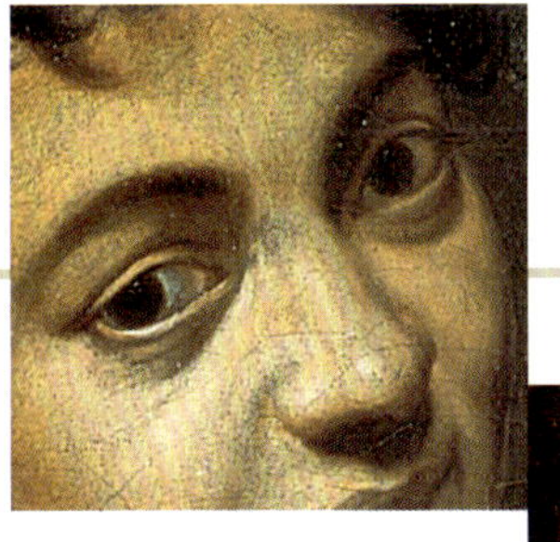

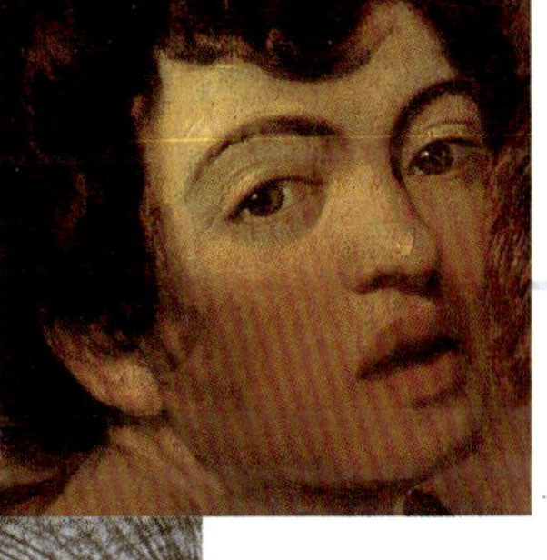

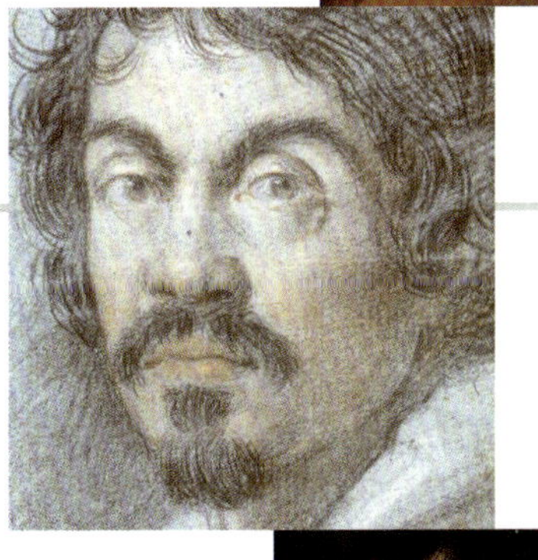

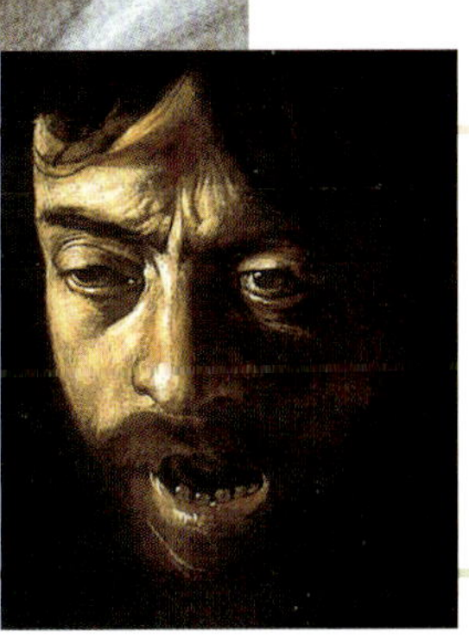

1571–1595

Beginnings in Milan and Rome

Birth and childhood in Milan and Caravaggio _ Apprenticeship under Simone Peterzano in Milan _ Death and bleak prospects _ Departure for Rome: hard times and illness _ Moving from workshop to workshop

Caravaggio is considered the pioneer of early modern painting. His œuvre includes eighty-seven definitively attributed works produced in twenty years of painting, and along with numerous genre pictures, they include a series of large-format altar paintings. Caravaggio's life was notable for intermittent acts of violence and conflicts with the law which constantly prompts scholars to seek parallels between his life and his work. The Biblical events with their acts of violence, and the darkness in some pictures, have been interpreted as an expression of the painter's emotional predisposition. Caravaggio's handling of subject matter was unconventional, as was his disregard for decorum, and his paintings thus provoked both admiration and sharp criticism from his contemporaries. He introduced secular and ugly elements alike into his religious scenes, and is particularly remembered as the inventor of *chiaroscuro*. This technique involves the use of hard light and deep shadow to achieve strong contrast in the modelling of the figures so that even simple events acquire a theatrical flourish. Known as 'naturalism', his style anticipated the work of many seventeenth-century European painters such as Juseppe Ribera and Diego Velázquez.

Birth and childhood in Milan and Caravaggio _ Michelangelo Merisi, who called himself after his home town Caravaggio, was born on 29 September 1571, probably in Milan in Lombardy, as the first of four children to Lucia Aratori and Fermo Merisi. Contemporary biographers say of the father that he worked as a master builder and architect for Francesco Sforza, the Marchese di Caravaggio. In 1576, the family fled from Milan to Caravaggio to escape the plague and continued to live there after the father's premature death that year.

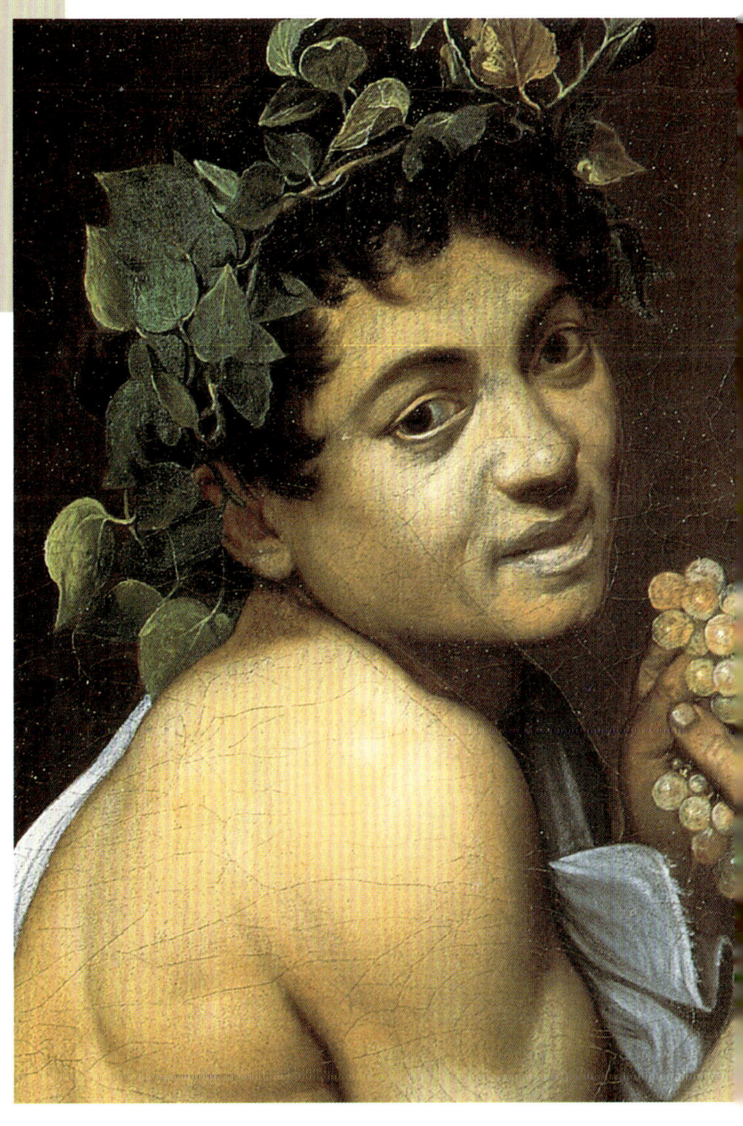

Self-portrait as the God of wine

Sick Little Bacchus (1593/94), detail, oil on canvas, 66 × 52 cm, Galleria Borghese, Rome

Simone Peterzano, **Deposition** (*c.* 1573–78), oil on canvas, 290 × 185 cm, S. Fedele, Milan

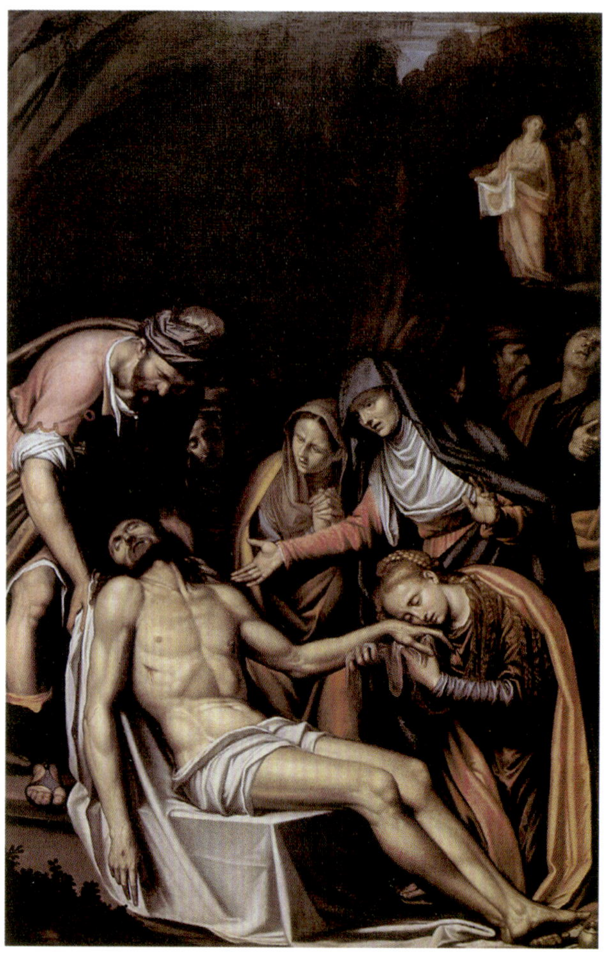

Apprenticeship under Simone Peterzano in Milan _ When he was nearly thirteen, Caravaggio entered Simone Peterzano's workshop in Milan on 6 April 1584, completing his training four years later. Peterzano was a painter from Bergamo whose works were described by the contemporary art writer Giovanni Paolo Lomazzo as having 'delicacy and charm'. Peterzano had trained in Venice and even

Influenced by Realist paintings

Vincenzo Campi, **Fruit Seller**, (*c.* 1580/81), oil on canvas, 145 × 215 cm, Brera, Milan

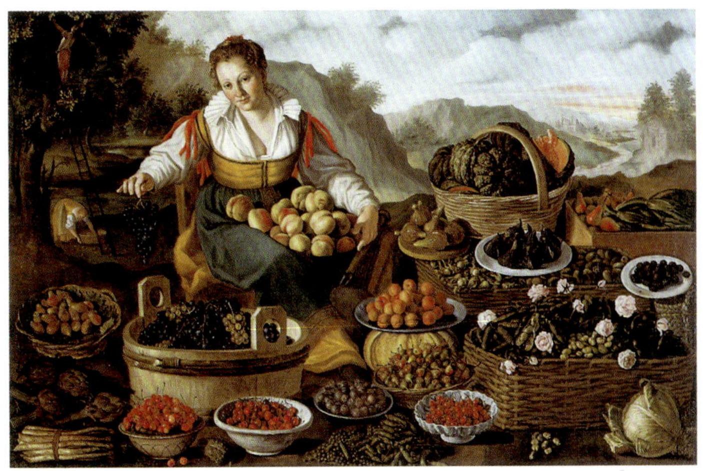

claimed to have been taught by Titian. Apart from the typical pronounced naturalism of the Lombard School, his paintings are notable for the forced, synthetic movement of forms and the strong colour contrasts of Mannerism.

Little is known about Caravaggio's apprenticeship. A look at his early paintings suggests that he was familiar with the works of Leonardo and Titian that were to be seen in Milan and had been impressed by them. The realistic paintings of Lombard artists such as

The Lombard School _ In the sixteenth century an artificial style of painting known as Mannerism prevailed virtually throughout Italy that increasingly moved away from nature as the prime model. Only the Lombard painters remain faithful to a traditional realist style, developing new effects in their handling of light and shadow and setting figures against a dark background, to be picked out with selective highlights. Among the most important representatives of the style were painters such as Vincenzo Foppa, Vincenzo Campi and Moretto di Brescia.

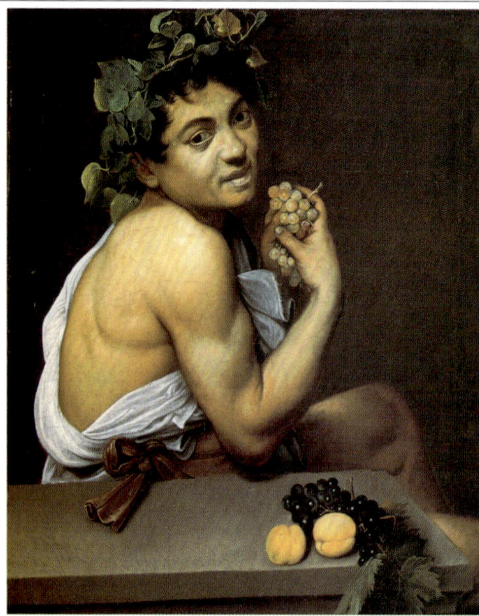

Self-Portrait as Bacchus (Sick Little Bacchus) (1593/94), oil on canvas, 66 × 52 cm, Galleria Borghese, Rome

the Campi brothers also had a great effect on Caravaggio. There is no documentary evidence that he went to Venice, but he was certainly familiar with Venetian painting from studying the works of painters from Brescia who were active in east Lombardy, such as Moroni and Giovanni Savoldo. These two closely followed Venetian painters Giorgione and Titian in the way they handled colour.

Death and bleak prospects _ On finishing his apprenticeship, Caravaggio returned to his home town. His mother died in 1590 and her estate was divided up among the children two years later. For this period there appear to be no positively attributable works and, as a consequence of epidemics and famine, prospects of commissions for painters were poor in Northern Italy. This resulted in a major exodus towards Rome where the art scene was flourishing under papal patronage. Like many others, Caravaggio, too, had presumably set off southwards in response to the precarious economic situation in the area he came from. En route, he is likely to have stopped in Parma – and probably also in Florence – to admire the local art treasures.

Caravaggio's Biography _ The events in Caravaggio's life are known to us from numerous reports by contemporaries. Among the most detailed are the accounts of Caravaggio and his (wrong)doings by art writers Giulio Mancini in *Considerazioni sulla pittura* (1619/20), Giovanni Baglione in *Le Vite de' Pittori, Scultori e Architetti* (1642) and Giovan Pietro Bellori in *Le Vite di Pittori, Scultori e Architetti moderni* (1672). These writers provide information not only about key biographical events, works and patrons but also describe his appearance and character, the latter being notoriously violent.

Departure for Rome: hard times and illness _ There is virtually no information about Caravaggio's early days in Rome. On his arrival there in 1592, the prospects were not very promising. For a while, the painter lived with Monsignor Pandolfo Pucci, who held a benefice at St Peter's and who commissioned him to copy devotional pictures in return for food and lodging. Pucci was probably an acquaintance through his uncle Ludovico, who was a priest and titular chaplain at S. Simpliciano in Milan. Fed up with a diet of salad, he left Pucci's house after a few months and took lodgings at the house of a Sicilian painter called Lorenzo, for whom he painted "heads for a groat apiece and produced three a day." Caravaggio did not stay there long either. All we know is that he lived in poverty during this time and continued to eke out a living from devotional pictures and copies. Concrete evidence exists that he then fell gravely ill with Roman fever which was spreading like wildfire across the whole country. There followed a six-month spell in the Ospedale della Consolazione, where he painted pictures for the prior, Monsignore Contreras, while recuperating. His first positively attributed picture, *Sick Little Bacchus* of 1593/94, dates from this period. Caravaggio used himself as a model for the god of wine.
Moving from workshop to workshop _ After he recovered, Caravaggio most probably spent some time with the Sienese painter Antiveduto Gramatica who had a flourishing studio. Gramatica was known as Gran Campocciante because of his great facility in painting heads and half-length figures. Caravaggio assisted him with this work

The Boy with a Basket of Fruit (1593/94), oil on canvas, 70 × 67 cm, Galleria Borghese, Rome

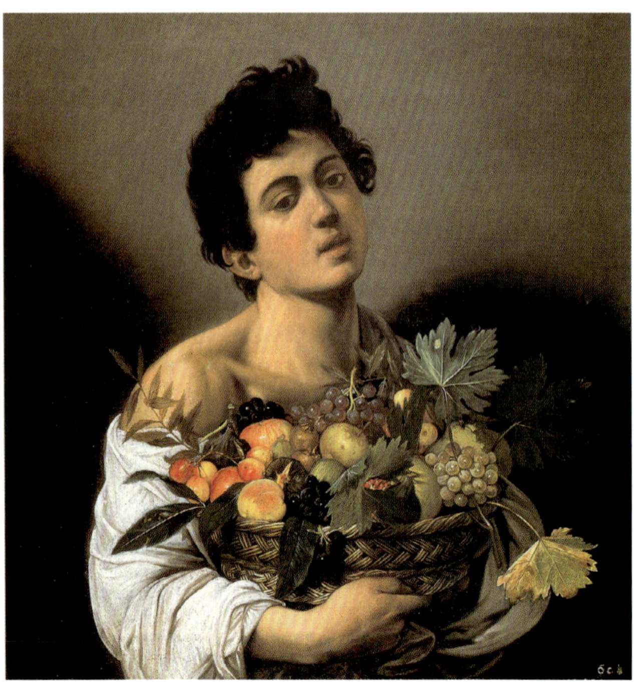

and thereby acquired the ability to commit figures to canvas as quickly as possible, a skill that would prove very useful to him later with his great altar commissions. However, he did not stay with Gramatica very long either.

In 1593, he is recorded as having spent around nine months in the workshop of Giuseppe Cesari, known as the Cavalier d'Arpino, who was one of the most successful painters in Rome at the time. His spell with Cesari was also significant for Caravaggio's subsequent career. The biographer Bellori reports that he painted 'fiori e frutti', i.e. still lifes with flowers and fruit. *The Boy with a Basket of Fruit* (1593/94) comes from the estate of the Cavalier d'Arpino and is thus likely to have been painted in his studio during this time.

The few paintings of the early years in Rome to survive are principally small-format gallery paintings with genre scenes and still lifes.

Intent to defraud

The Fortune-Teller (*c.* 1598/99), oil on canvas, 99 × 131 cm, Louvre, Paris

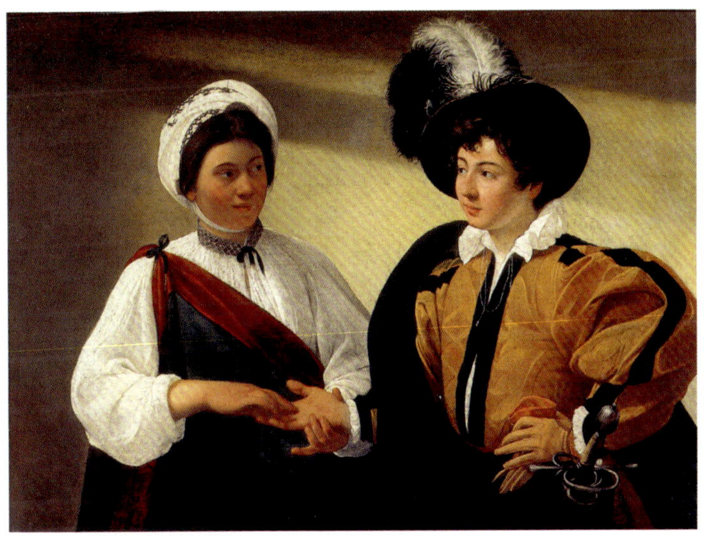

Encouraged by a painter friend, Prospero Orsi, he did pictures with genre-type subjects, including *The Fortune-Teller*. Caravaggio showed himself here as an observer with a penchant for irony, depicting the fortune-teller unobtrusively removing the ring from the dandy's finger as she tells his fortune. These paintings make him a successor to the Bolognese painter Annibale Carracci, who painted *The Bean Eater* around 1584.

Everyday activities as the subject

Annibale Carracci, The Bean Eater (*c.* 1584), oil on canvas, Palazzo Colonna, Rome

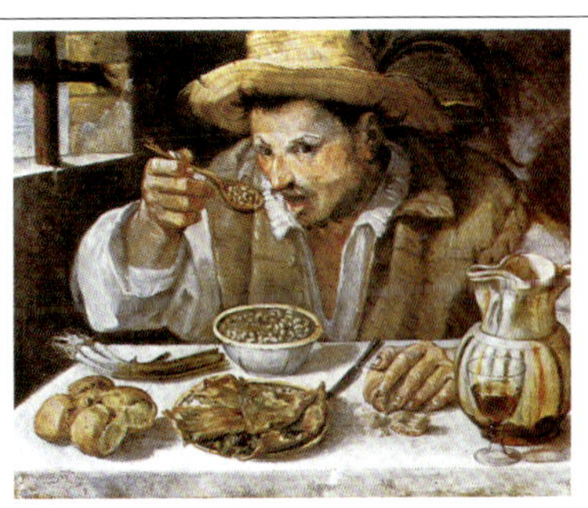

Boy Bitten by a Lizard (1595), oil on canvas, 65.8 × 52.3 cm,
Fondazione Roberto Longhi, Florence

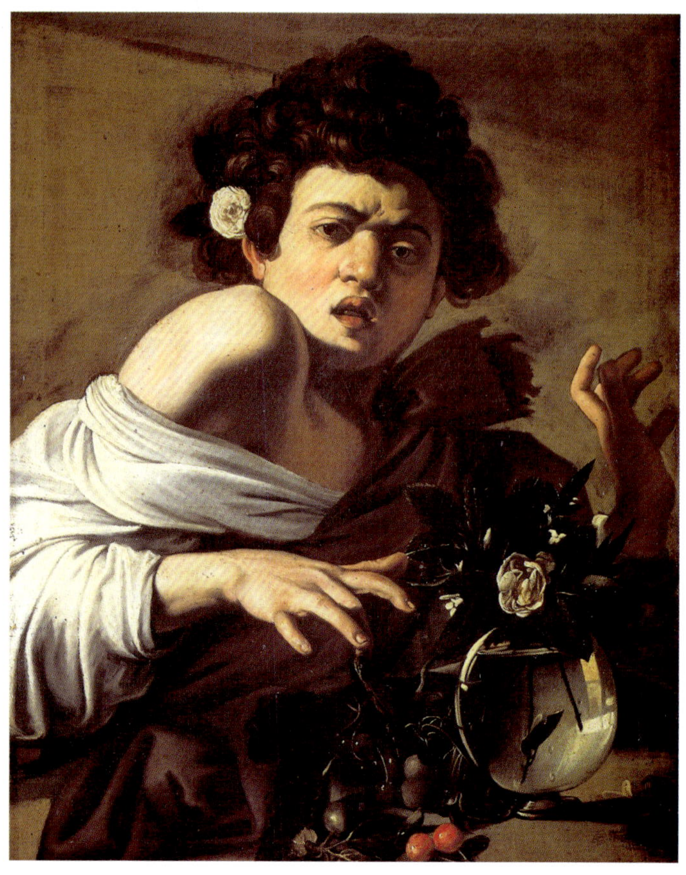

The subject of another genre painting, *Boy Bitten by a Lizard* of 1595, is said to imitate a famous motif in a drawing by Sofonisba Anguissola, showing her son bitten by a crab. With his depiction of a boy recoiling with pain after having being bitten by a lizard, Caravaggio reveals his interest in extreme depictions of emotional outbursts. The picture was interpreted as a moral warning about the dangers of life or the pain that follows lust, or even as an allegory of the wound that love deals.

A similar subject painted realistically

Sofonisba Anguissola, **Portrait of Her Son Asdrubale, Nipped by a Crab** (*c.* 1554), black chalk on paper, 33.3 × 38.5 cm, Museo di Capodimonte, Naples

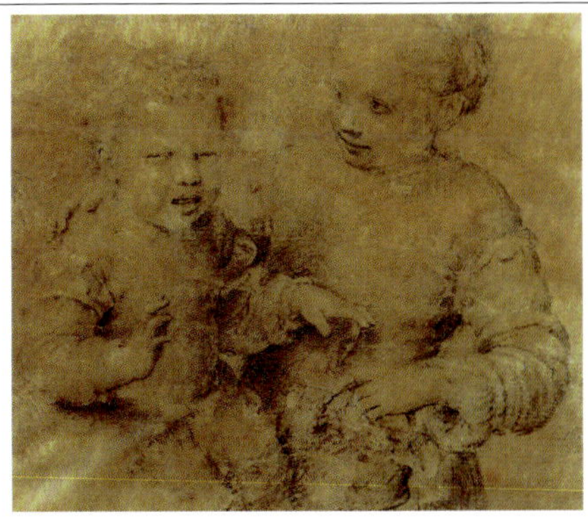

It was only after being pressed by the French art dealer Maestro Valentino that Caravaggio finally turned to religious subjects as well and painted *St Francisof Assisi in Ecstasy*. The angel is shown as a seductive youth, with the entranced saint lying in his arms. Caravaggio's interpretation of the scene is unusual because of the intimacy between St Francis and the angel.

Shocking intimacy between the saint and the angel

St Francis of Assisi in Ecstasy (*c.* 1596), oil on canvas, 92.5 × 127.8 cm, Wadsworth Atheneum, Hartford

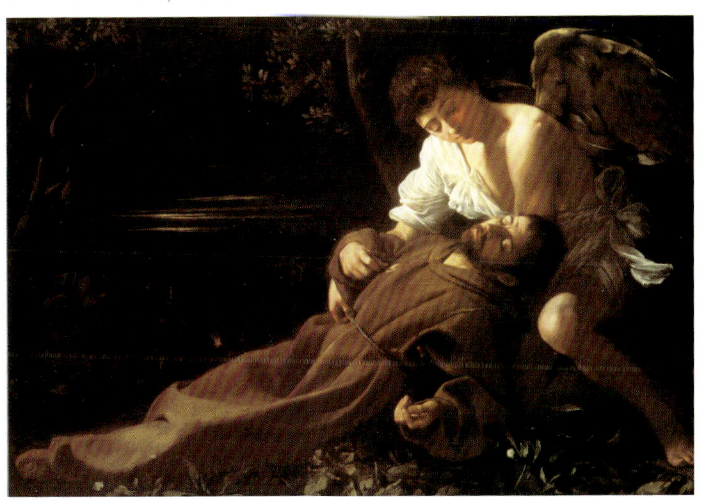

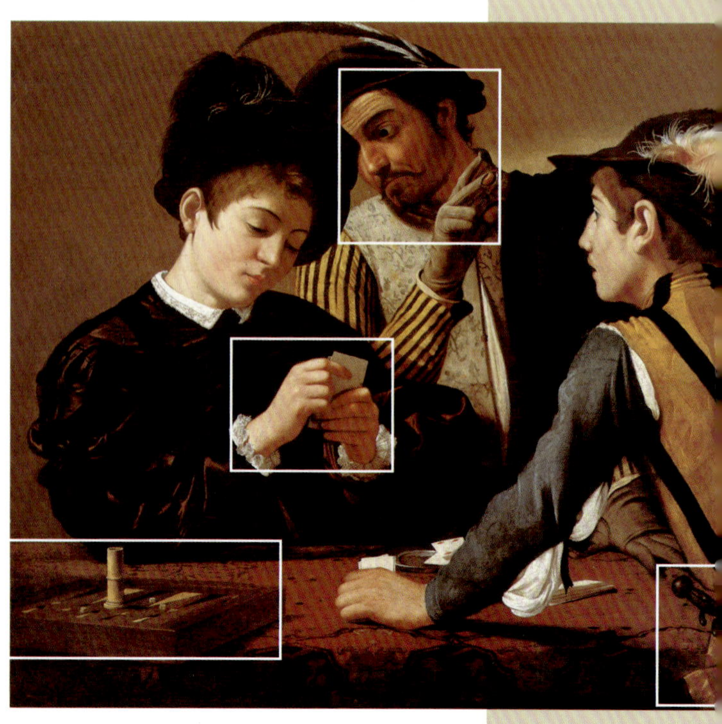

The Cardsharps (1595), oil on canvas, 94.2 × 131.3 cm, Kimbell Art Museum, Fort Worth

The Cardsharps

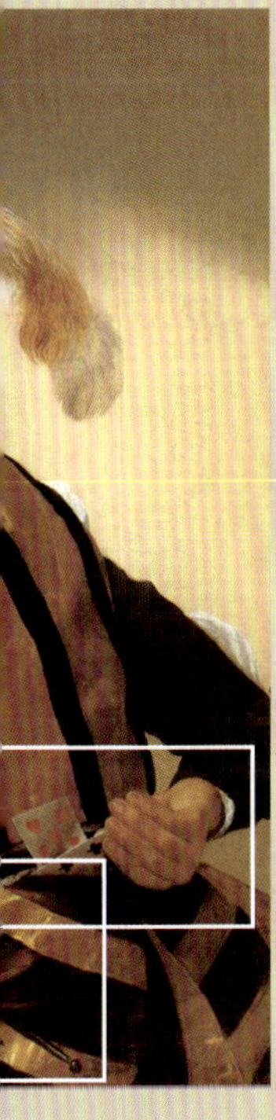

Cheats and murderers _ Caravaggio takes genre painting in Italy forward

The painting of *The Cardsharps* of 1595 is one of the genre paintings that Caravaggio completed during his time at Cavaliere d'Arpino's studio. It was the first of the painter's works his later patron Cardinal del Monte acquired for his collection from the dealer Maestro Valentino.

The subject matter was unusual and was first popularised in Italy by Caravaggio. The scene is of three men playing cards, with one of the three obviously being taken for a ride by the other two. They are playing *primero*, a precursor of poker. The naive-looking young man, dressed elegantly in black and red velvet sitting frontally to the viewer, is absorbed in his cards and still hesitating over his move while, behind him, an older man with threadbare gloves is standing, looking over his shoulder. The latter has stretched out three fingers of his left hand to flag information about the youth's cards to the player opposite. The cheating player, likewise very young and shabbily dressed, can only be seen from behind. He follows the sign given to him and is about to pull out one of the cards he has hidden behind him in his waistband, thus bettering his hand and will subsequently win the game.

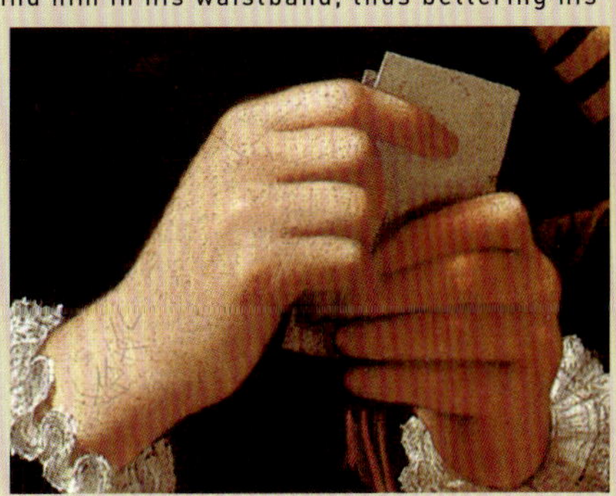

The setting in which the game takes place is not depicted in detail. The focus is on a confined space around a table covered with an ornate rug. In front, the edge of the

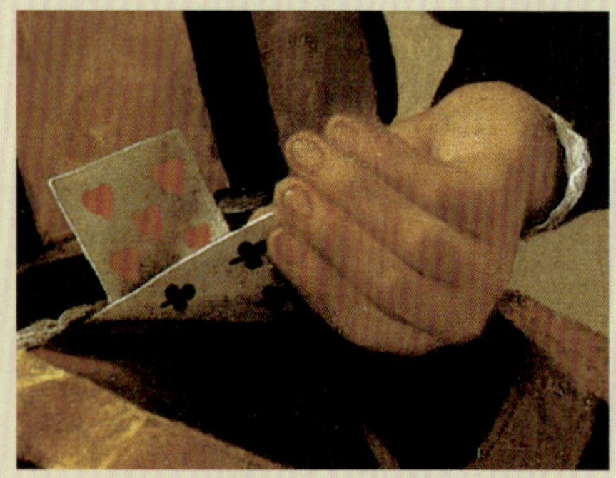

table defines the border, while to the right the painter extends the pictorial space by means of light. Dice, dice shakers and backgammon indicate that other games have been played or are still to take place. The viewer is given no indication as to the stakes – no money or other objects are shown that could provide a clue. The cheating obviously taking place in the game suggests that the scene is set in a seedy or even criminal location. The dagger that the young cheat has ready to hand in his waistband indicates that violence was not an uncommon way of solving conflicts in this milieu. His dress and weapon distinguish him as a *bravo* – a person hired to carry out certain deeds armed with a dagger or rapier.

The Cardsharps has been interpreted as a parable of innocence and deceit. Admittedly, everything indicates that the cheats will be successful. The player concentrating on his hand has noticed neither the gestures of the man behind him nor does he heed what his opponent is doing. While in Netherlandish paintings of similar subjects the focus is on praising good and condemning evil, Caravaggio takes no moral stance. At best, the frontal view of the 'good' player, his regular features and better dress versus the rear view of his opponent, the shabby clothing of the two cheats and their slightly distorted facial features, may be interpreted in a moral sense. The painter, however, was mainly interested in the study of physiognomies, portraying the lively

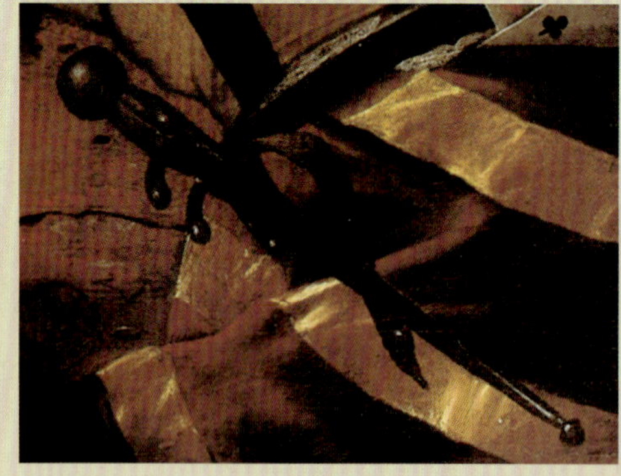

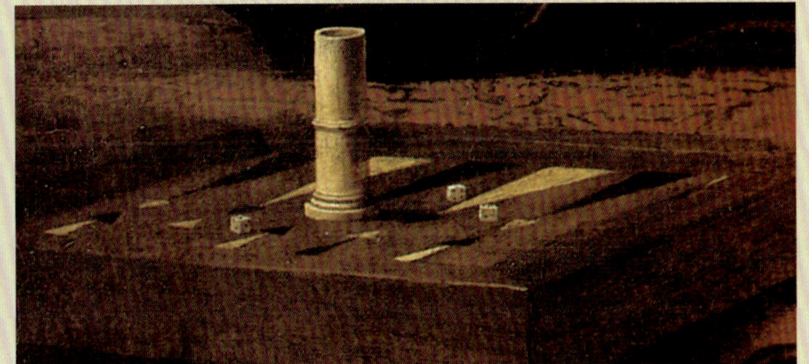

facial expressions and gestures of the figures, emphasising their faces and hands with the careful use of intensive light. The face of the frowning older player in particular, with his wrinkled forehead, wide-open eyes and tight lips, is a study of a momentary emotional expression and suspense.

In *Boy Bitten by a Lizard* Caravaggio had already focused on capturing the features of a face distorted by pain in as much detail as possible. The painter's treatment of pictorial space, the positioning of the figures, the choice of models and their often unflattering traits, together with the violent gestures and expressions of saintly figures in his later altar paintings, was similarly unconventional, and led to his works being repeatedly rejected by his contemporaries. However, *The Cardsharps* enjoyed great popularity, as over thirty existing copies would suggest. According to Bellori's account, it was particularly this work that prompted Cardinal del Monte to take Caravaggio into his household.

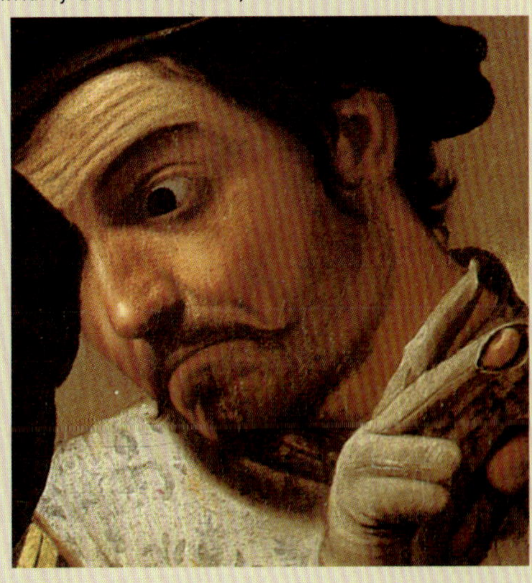

1595–1600

Productive Years and Prominent Patrons

Music as bewitchment of the senses _ Homoeroticism or friendship _ Genre pictures and still lifes _ Unconventional handling of religious themes

Caravaggio made the acquaintance of Cardinal Francesco Maria del Monte through the French art dealer Maestro Valentino who had a shop near the church of S. Luigi dei Francesi. The cardinal showed interest in his paintings and invited him to his palazzo. Del Monte was the Tuscan ambassador to the Holy See and moved in the most exclusive circles in the Vatican. After the numerous changes of abode since he moved to Rome, the period in del Monte's household from 1595 was a peaceful and decidedly productive time. The painter spent five years at the Palazzo Madama as a member of the Cardinal's *famiglia*, working for him and enjoying his patronage. Del Monte had unlimited access to the world of art lovers in Rome with money to spend, and could introduce the artist to them. During these years, Caravaggio did a number of genre pictures with musicians, still lifes, portraits of youths disguised as Bacchus and paintings of religious subjects for collectors, as well as monumental altar pictures. His clients were cardinals such as Matteo Contarelli, aristocrats like the Giustinianis and financiers including Ottavio Costa, all of them associated with Cardinal del Monte.

Music as a bewitchment of the senses _ Cardinal del Monte had not only had a humanist education but was also a great music lover, and the subjects involving music in Caravaggio's œuvre can be attributed to his influence.

One of these was the painting *The Musicians*, commissioned by the Cardinal. The scene is of four youths, three of whom are making music. One plays the lute, another the horn and the third sings from sheet music. The fourth boy in the background, whose wings originally identifying him as Cupid were later overpainted, is breaking off grapes

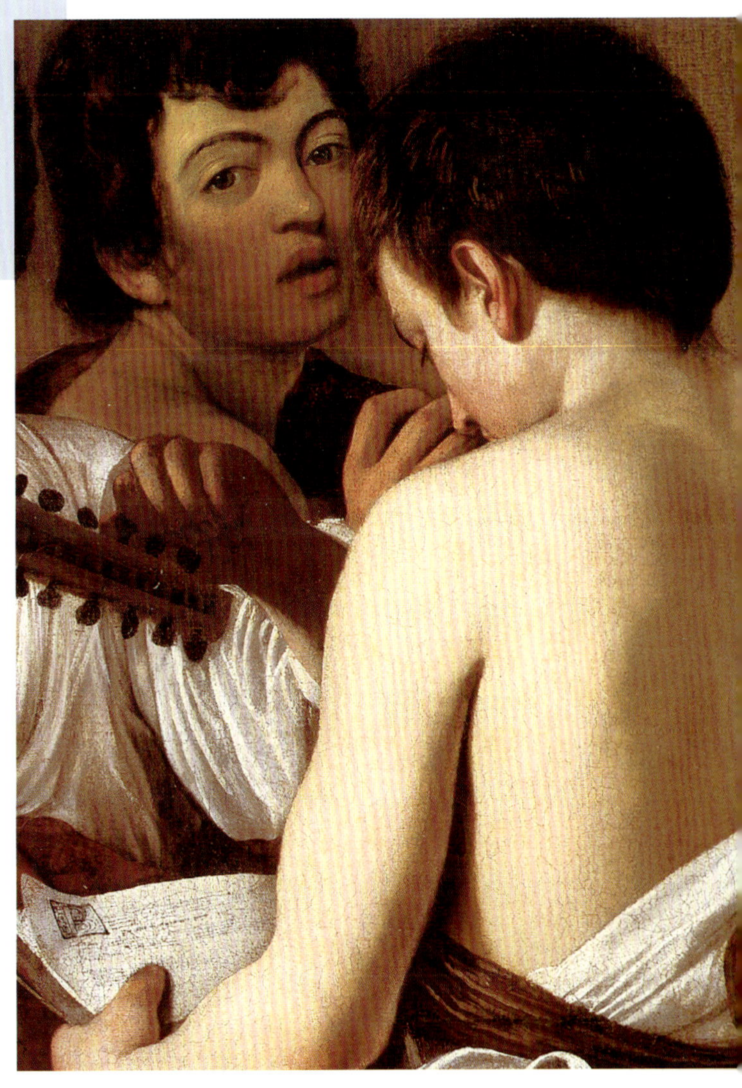

A hidden self-portrait as a horn player

The Musicians (*c.* 1595), detail, oil on canvas, 87.9 × 115.9 cm, Metropolitan Museum of Art, New York

Caravaggio's patron

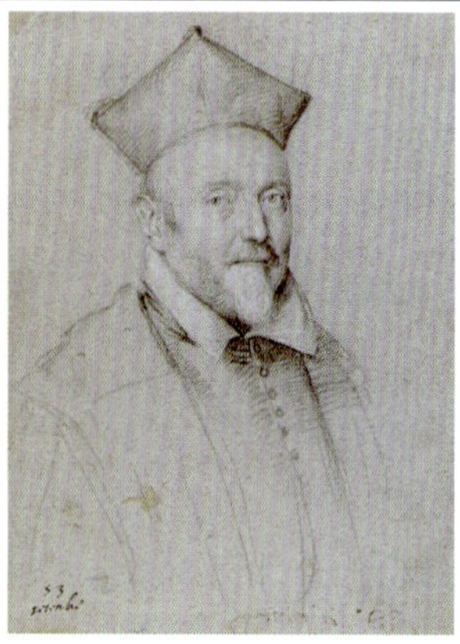

Ottavio Leoni, **Portrait of Francesco Maria del Monte** (1618), black chalk with white highlights on blue paper, 22.8 × 16.5 cm, John and Mable Ringling Museum of Art, Sarasota

from a bunch. The horn player in the background is thought to be a self-portrait of Caravaggio.

There are two versions of *The Lute Player* whose androgynous figure is often taken to be a female: one was painted for del Monte, the other for the banker Vincenzo Giustiniani. The subject of love is

The erotic connotation of music

The Musicians (*c.* 1595), oil on canvas, 87.9 × 115.9 cm, Metropolitan Museum of Art, New York

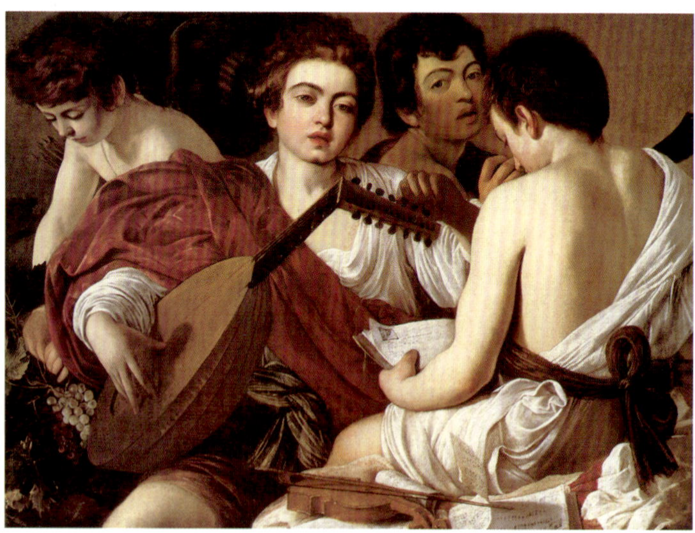

explicitly alluded to in the sheet music, which is open at *Voi sapete ch'io vi amo* (You know I love you). This is a quote from a madrigal by the French composer Jacques Arcadelt.

Homoeroticism or friendship _ It has been assumed from Caravaggio's preference for scenes of purely male society and provocative boys that the artist moved in a homoerotic milieu. In support of this thesis is not only the sensual expressions and soft bodies of the naked

Androgynous figure

The Lute Player (*c.* 1595/96), oil on canvas, 94 × 119 cm, Hermitage, St Petersburg

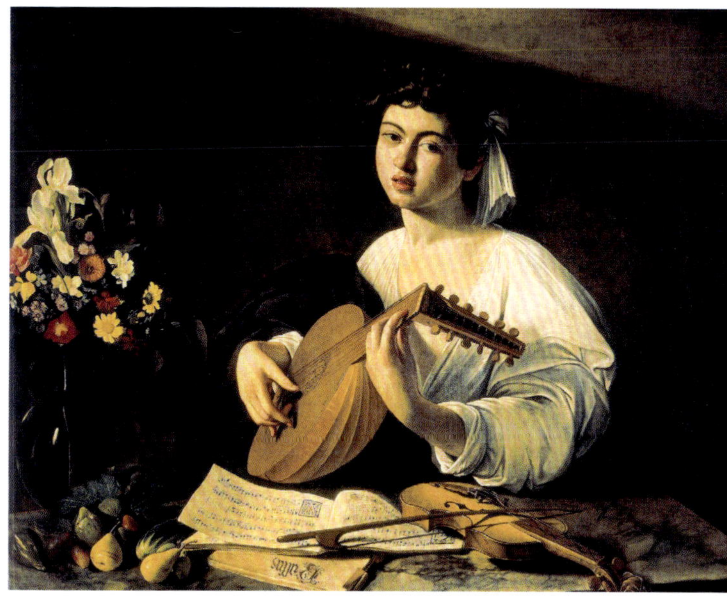

or nearly naked boys crowded together, but also the appearance of love as a subject matter both in *The Musicians* and in *Victorious Cupid* (see p. 42f.). Music as a system of harmony but also as sound bewitching the senses has been associated with love since time immemorial. In *The Musicians*, love and friendship bind the youths together, as the presence of Cupid breaking off a grape in the background suggests, again an indication of the erotic connotation of music. Some scholars make much of Caravaggio's (homo)sexuality in their interpretation of his works. However, at that time, homosexuality was

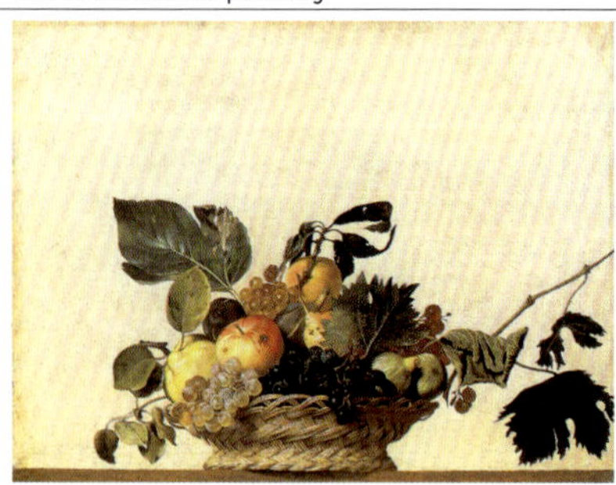

Basket of Fruit (*c.* 1601), oil on canvas, 31 × 47 cm, Pinacoteca Ambrosiana, Milan

not seen as anything to set someone apart, nor was it considered to have any relevance to a person's identity. Today's prevailing sharp distinction between eroticism, homoeroticism and friendship is a recent phenomenon that does not predate modern lifestyles and legislative practice, and cannot be applied indiscriminately to the Early Modern period.

Genre pictures and still lifes _ During this same period Caravaggio continued to work on other genre paintings and still lifes. The painting of the young Bacchus, with his realistically depicted, sunburnt face and ingrained hands contrasting with the paler skin of the upper body, is more to do with a youth who normally wears clothes, thus only exposing his head and hands to the sun, and who agreed to

Still Life in Italy _ The genesis of the still life as a painting genre in Italy is attributed to the demand by the Counter-Reformation for a strict separation between religious and secular motifs in paintings. In response to this demand, painters decided to make groups of objects into subject matter and arrange them into a harmonious unity, painting objects or dead animals from nature. As the high prices paid prove, it was a genre that collectors very much appreciated. Nonetheless, in the academic hierarchy of genres, still lifes ranked lowest beneath history painting and portrait painting, on the grounds that its aim was pure *imitatio*.

Young man with sunburnt hands

Bacchus (*c.* 1597), oil on canvas, 95 × 85 cm, Uffizi, Florence

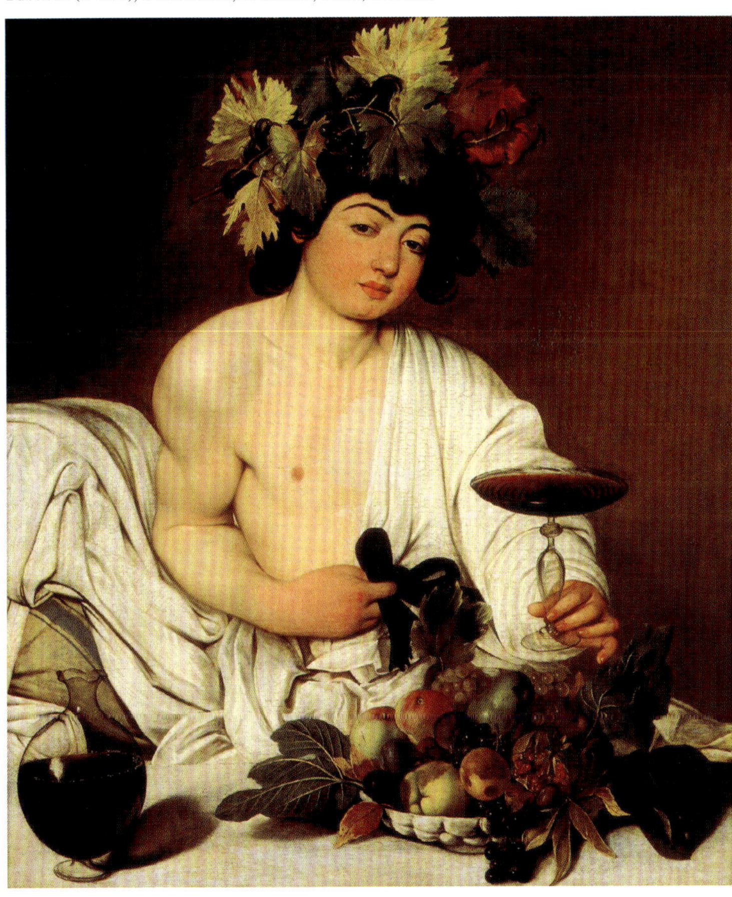

pose as the god of wine, than with a convincing picture of Bacchus himself.

Basket of Fruit is attributed particular importance in Caravaggio's œuvre as scholars rank it as the first still life. In the Bacchus picture, the god also has a bowl of fruit in front of him whereas, in this representation, the basket of fruit itself is the sole subject. Caravaggio does not even suggest the edge of the table but shows the woven fruit basket on a brown line. It contains grapes and figs, a lemon, a pear,

With the features of an ordinary woman

Repentent Magdalene (*c.* 1595/96), oil on canvas, 122.5 × 98.5 cm, Galleria Doria Pamphilj, Rome

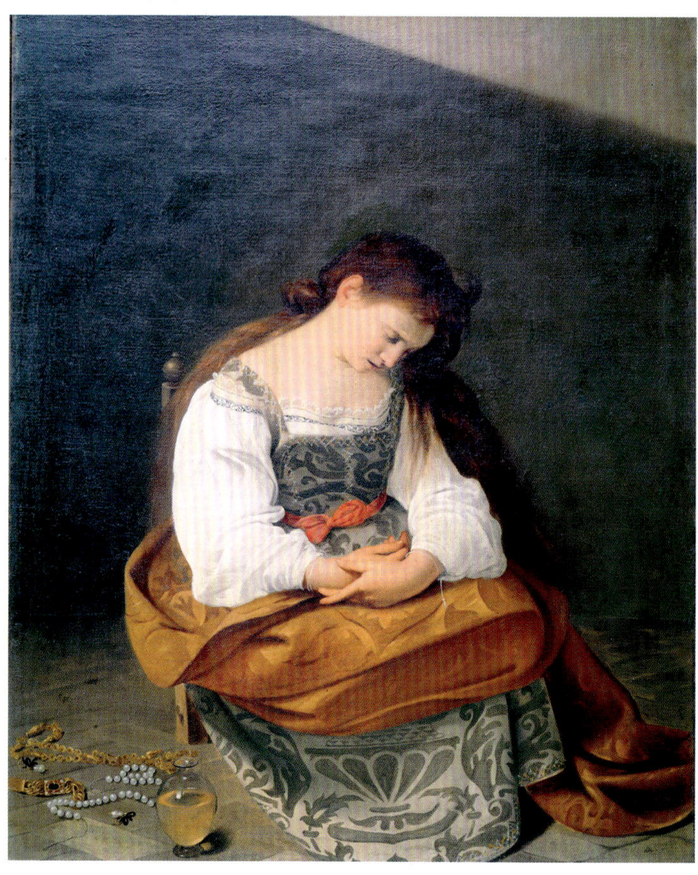

an apple and a peach, all framed with vine leaves. The maggoty apple and the sometimes withered vine leaves allude to the transitoriness of things mortal. Caravaggio turned the basket into a virtuoso illusion – or *trompe l'œil* – itself by making it project out of the picture, turning the painted object into something virtually real.

Unconventional handling of religious themes _ Post-1595, Caravaggio took to painting religious subjects, which up to that time had hardly featured in his œuvre. In *Repentant Magdalene*, Magdalene sits on a low stool as a despised sinner with a disreputable past, her hands folded in her lap and her head bowed in contrition. On the ground, the saint's chains, jewellery and a pot of ointment are artfully arranged. All these indicate that the painter obviously saw Mary Magdalene as a sinner not in her unchastity, like most painters of the time, but in her vanity. In her melancholy contemplation, the young woman conveys an expression of human tragedy

Like his *Repentant Magdalene*, Caravaggio painted *Rest on the Flight to Egypt* for the papal official Gerolamo Vittrici. The foreground of the painting contains a music-making angel who has his back turned to the viewer and is playing a fiddle with a broken string. Strict geometry divides the painting in two halves each side of the angel. On the left a grey-haired Joseph clasps the music book while, on the right, Mary is holding the Child close to her, both of them asleep. The fantastic landscape in which the scene is set is both impressive and rare in Caravaggio, and is notably pastoral. On the left, the stony ground and

An unclothed angel stands in mid-painting

Rest on the Flight into Egypt (*c.* 1595), oil on canvas, 135 × 166.5 cm, Galleria Doria Pamphilj, Rome

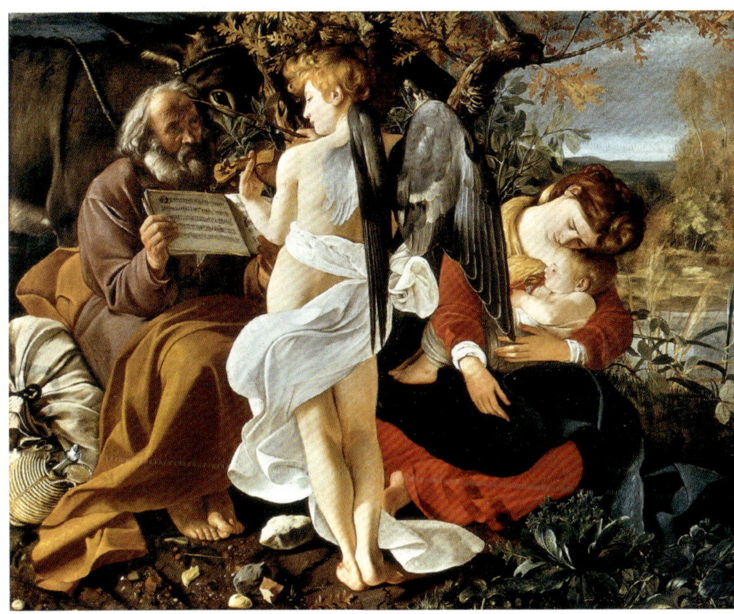

Judith Beheading Holofernes (*c.* 1599), oil on canvas, 145 × 195 cm, Galleria Nazionale d'Arte Antica, Rome

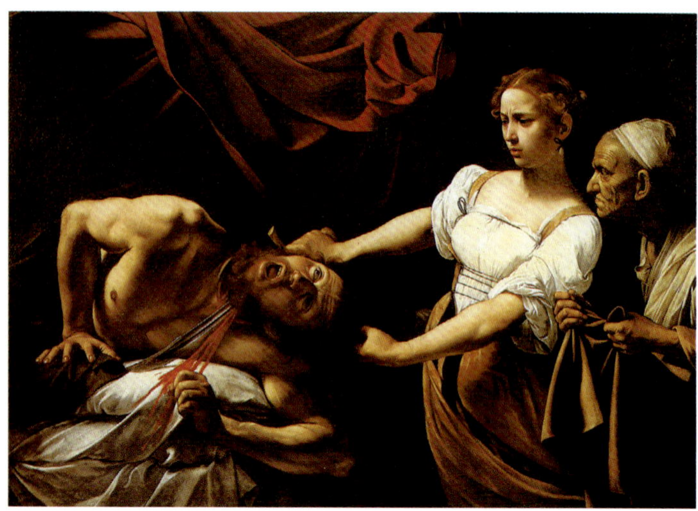

barrenness around the elderly Joseph symbolise infertility and age. On the right, the Virgin with the Child represent eternal life and youth in the middle of a paradisiacal landscape with flowers. The same young woman with red hair seems to have posed for the figure of Mary as for *Repentant Magdalene*, and the vitality in the figure of the child also suggests a live model.

Another painting from Caravaggio's time in Cardinal del Monte's household is *Judith Beheading Holofernes*, a Biblical scene of particular brutality that would subsequently inspire numerous imitations. The commission came from Ottavio Costa. The moment Caravaggio chose for the picture is when the lovely Israelite widow Judith of Bethulia beheads Holofernes, the king of the Assyrian army besieging her city, having previously pretended to yield to his importunities. Whereas Judith had previously been interpreted as the Biblical saviour of the chosen people, Caravaggio introduces the raw violence of her action into the scene. It is not clear from her facial expression whether beauty and comeliness are uppermost or savagery and cruelty.

Caravaggio's Models _ Whereas with other painters of the era, only family members generally can be identified as models, with Caravaggio it was different. As the similar features of different figures in several paintings prove, he always made use of the same models, and some of them are known to us by name. For example, Fillide Melandrei, a courtesan of whom he painted a now lost portrait, sat for three pictures – as the saint in *St Catherine of Alexandria*, Martha in *The Conversion of Mary Magdalene* and Judith in *Judith Beheading Holofernes*. The facial features of fellow painter Mario Minniti, with whom he shared a studio, recur in both *The Lute Player* and *The Musicians*.

In the picture of *St Catherine of Alexandria* for Costa the banker, Caravaggio was more conventional. As in *Judith*, the model was the courtesan Fillide Melandrei. Shown here with her attributes of a wheel, sword and martyr's palm, the princess from Alexandria had defied martyrdom by breaking the wheel of torture to which she had been bound, resulting in her execution with a sword.

A princess defies martyrdom

St Catherine of Alexandria
(c. 1599), oil on canvas, 173 × 133 cm,
Museo Thyssen-Bornemisza, Madrid

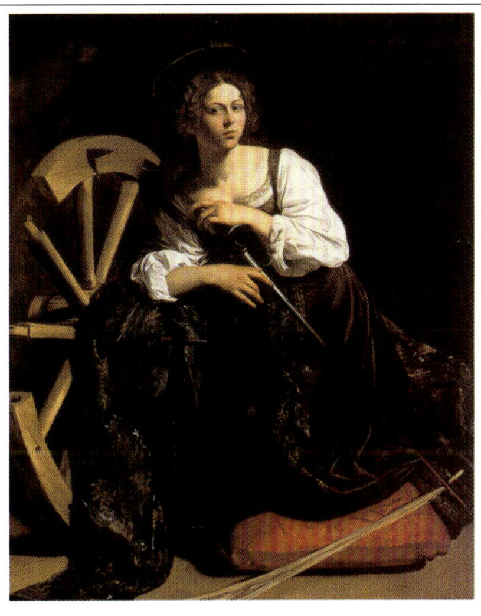

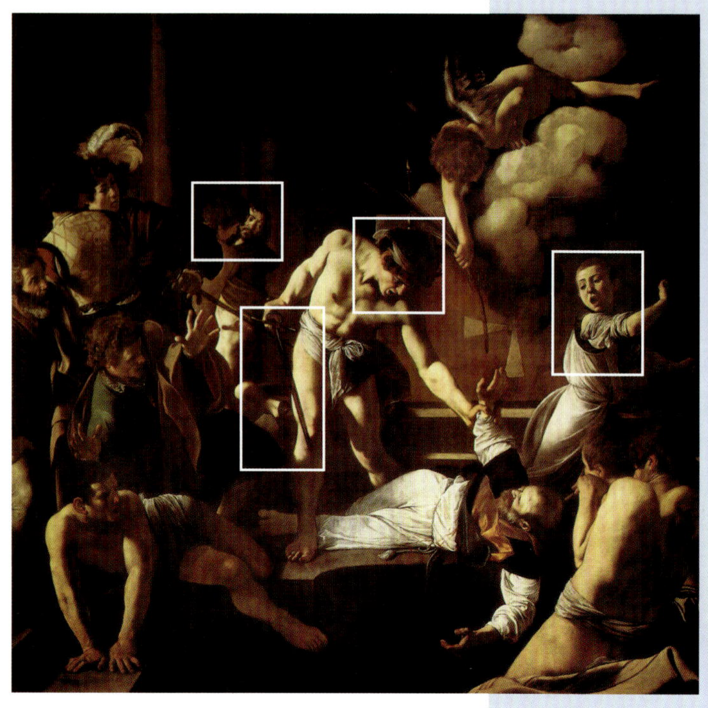

The Martyrdom of St Matthew (1600), oil on canvas, 323 × 343 cm, S. Luigi dei Francesi, Rome

The Martyrdom of St Matthew

The martyrdom of a saint as a dramatic event _ Caravaggio's first large-format altar painting

On 23 July 1599, Caravaggio signed a contract for two altar paintings for the Contarelli Chapel in San Luigi dei Francesi, the French national church in Rome. It was his first major contract, and he had won it through the good offices of Cardinal del Monte, who had excellent contacts among the French. As part of the planned refurbishing of the church, Cardinal Matteo Contarelli had acquired a chapel and he intended to fit it out with due ostentation, dedicating it to his patron saint. Caravaggio was contracted to execute two large-format paintings of the martyrdom and calling of St Matthew. He completed them within a few months, so that they were already installed by July 1600.

As reported in the Apocrypha, the Apostle Matthew had converted Egippus, the king of Ethiopia, to Christianity. His successor Hirtacus had designs on his daughter Iphigenia. Conflict followed, as Matthew had elicited a vow of chastity from her, and she publicly repudiated the new king in church. The latter took his revenge by having the apostle murdered during the service.

Caravaggio depicts Matthew being interrupted as he administered the service and his subsequent death as a martyr. The setting is on the steps to a Christian altar, on which a candle burns, the front of the altar being marked with a Greek cross. Because of the steps leading up on the left, some scholars have identified a font at the front, with the half-naked men in the foreground looking at it. The centre of the picture is occupied not by the saint but by his killer, who has adopted an almost Herculean pose to slay St Matthew with his sword as he lies in front of him. He holds him by the right wrist to keep in position for the fatal blow. St Matthew is wearing a chasuble and has raised his outstretched arm in a sweeping defensive gesture towards the murderer, whom he gazes at fearlessly with raised head. A wound and blood on the saint's chest show that he has already been struck once. An angel on a cloud above is ready to hand the saint the martyr's palm. Caravaggio thus integrates the heavenly reward of martyrdom and thereby the other-worldly meaning of the event into the narrative itself.

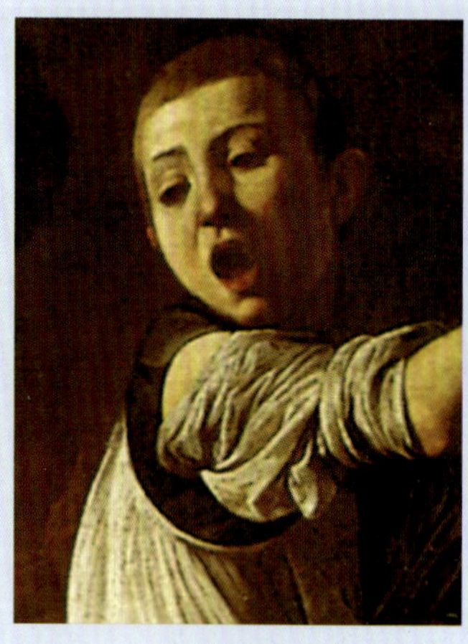

Standing over the defenceless saint with triumphant mien, the half-naked killer with the sword obviously embodies bestiality. The crudeness of his nakedness is quite distinct from the other nude figures of Caravaggio such as Cupid, Bacchus and the musicians, who are all charming and comely to look at. Likewise the facial expression of the killer, who looks down at the saint with a hate-distorted grimace, emphasises the tone of violence that predominates in the picture.

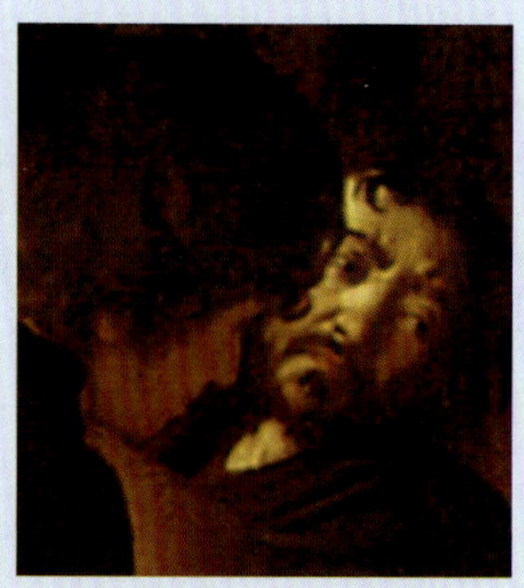

The painting is divided into two zones by the killer/saint group. The goodies are obviously on the right, represented by the boy fleeing with horror and the two half-naked men, who similarly writhe in consternation. The visibly agitated boy had been a server at the service. By reflecting the brutality of the beheading in the emotional figure of the boy, Caravaggio doubles the force of the act. The two half-naked *ignudi* seem to be merged into a single figure with two heads facing away from us, virtually superimposed on top of each other. They have the function of *repoussoir* figures, leading the viewer's eye from the real into the fictional arena of the event depicted in the painting.

On the left-hand side of the painting are two separate groups. In the lower zone are several men also obviously shaken by the murder. In contrast, the upper zone is filled with a group of baddies – four young men running away. This group making off includes a good-looking youth

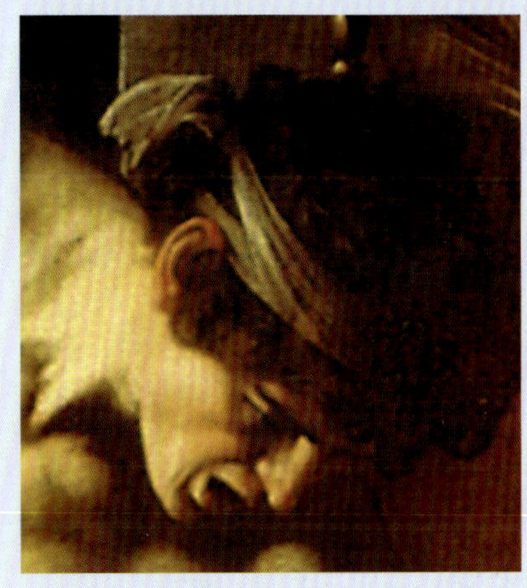

with a plume on his cap, who looks the apostle in the face once more, while thrusting his sword back into its sheath. He is the one who, according to legend, ran the saint through from behind and is now running away. There is thus a second murderer involved in the event beside the killer. Caravaggio distinguishes these men by their dress and weapons as *bravos*, i.e. hired assassins. Caravaggio has also depicted himself among the baddies. The figure on the left of the killer behind the crossed sword has been identified with Caravaggio because of the similarity with the portrait of the artist by Ottavio Leoni. Half hidden, but with a sharply lit lower body, he is the only one of those making off to show his broad face front on. Likewise, as the only one to turn to look back at the beheading, he hints at a psychological reaction. With his short beard and tortured facial expression, perhaps even sorrow, he is there as a witness to the martyrdom of St Matthew.

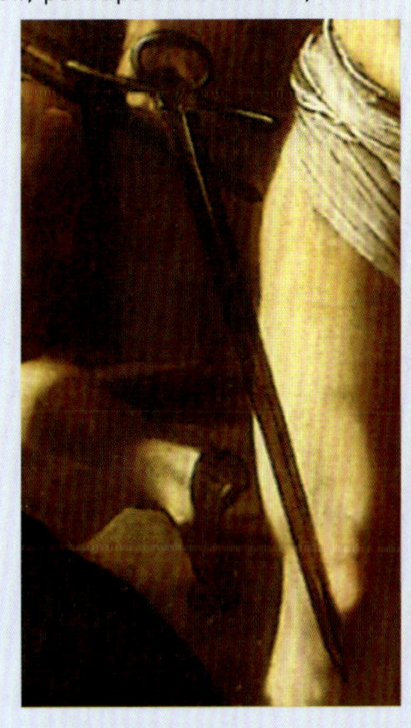

Caravaggio's unconventional interpretation of the event is also clearly evident in the way the scene is depicted not as a martyrdom in any way but, in its brutality, as an assassination. X-ray photos of the painting show how the artist developed what was originally a relatively static scene such as we find in works from the High Renaissance into a highly dramatic event by making considerable changes in the composition and gestures of the figures involved.

1600–1606

Violence and Genius

Constant conflict with the law _ Altar pictures and other problems _ Caravaggio as a storyteller _ Deadly games

Constant conflict with the law _ Caravaggio stayed in Cardinal del Monte's peaceful household until late autumn 1600. After leaving his patron, he remained in Rome for another six years, but during this time was in constant conflict with the law. From May 1600, excellent documentary evidence for his wrongdoings can be found in the form of regular entries in the archives of the Roman magistrates. Except for one instance where he was trying to mediate in a quarrel, the incidents all involve acts of violence, and he was had up for stabbings, brawling, disturbing the peace, verbal abuse of all kinds, defamation of character, possessing offensive weapons and the like. He was hauled before the court and arrested a number of times.

That Caravaggio was not on good terms even with fellow artists is indicated by proceedings against him instituted by Giovanni Baglione. On 28 August 1603, Baglione initiated an action against Caravaggio and three other artists – the painters Orazio Gentileschi and Filippo Trisegno and the architect Onorio Longhi – for defamation of character and circulating slanderous poems. Caravaggio was subsequently arrested on 11 September and taken to Tor di Nona prison. Baglione accused the painter of having written and distributed two slanderous sonnets so as to publicly mock him. In his statement, he claimed that Caravaggio was envious of his success with the altar painting of the *Resurrection* in the church of Il Gesù, Rome. In his counterstatement, Caravaggio rejected the accusations, laying into his opponent and his artistic capabilities in no uncertain terms: At one point, he says: "I do not know of a single painter who praises Giovanni Baglione as a talented artist." After the French ambassador interceded with the Holy See on the painter's behalf, Caravaggio was released on 25 September 1603.

Altar pictures and other problems _ Del Monte made a further significant contribution to Caravaggio's career by helping him to win

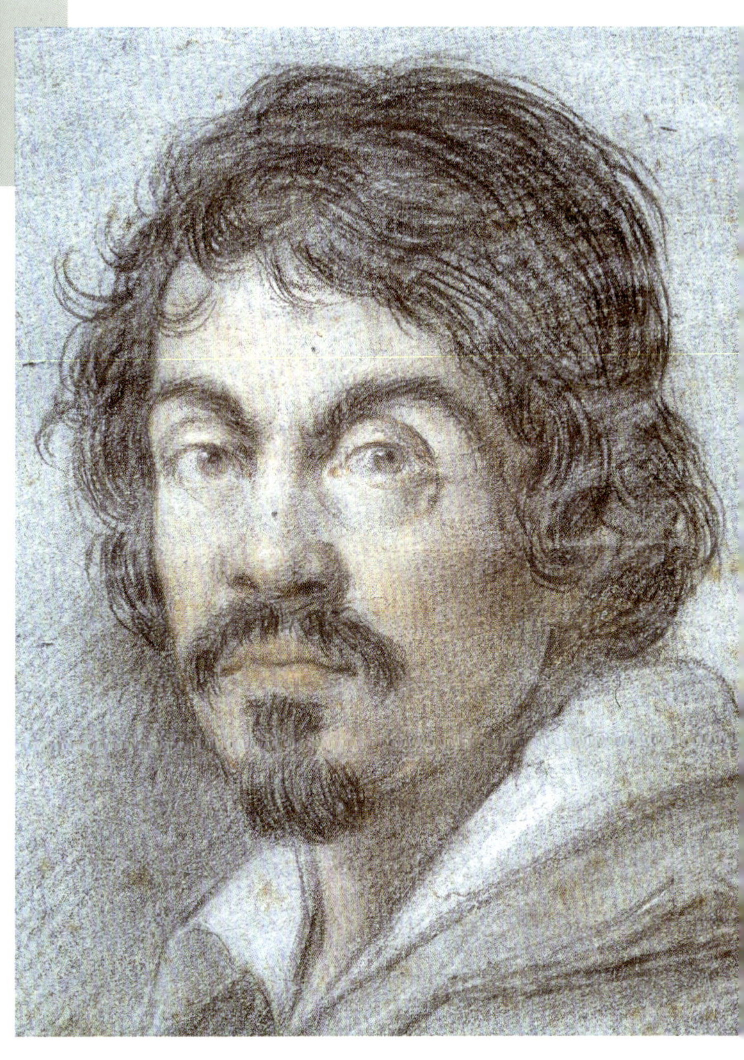

A fellow artist paints Caravaggio's portrait

Ottavio Leoni, **Portrait of Caravaggio** (*c.* 1621–25), red and white chalk, with white highlights on blue paper, 23.4 × 16.3 cm, Biblioteca Marucelliana, Florence

The Calling of St Matthew (1600), oil on canvas, 322 × 340 cm, S. Luigi dei Francesi, Rome

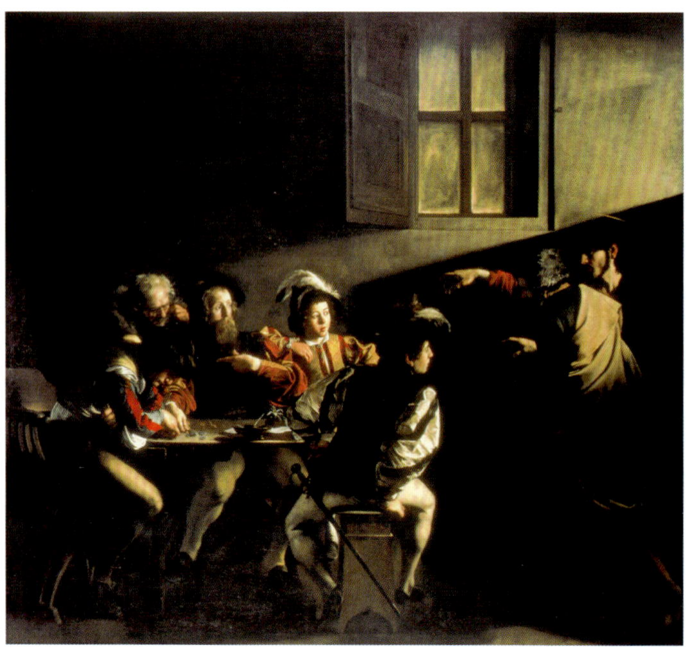

his first major commission, the altar paintings of *The Calling of St Matthew* and *The Martyrdom of St Matthew* for the Contarelli Chapel in S. Luigi dei Francesi in Rome. In the *Calling of St Matthew*, Jesus and Peter are seen entering the tax collector's office and calling on him to join them. Which figure is Matthew – the young man at the left end of the table who goes on counting money or the dominant figure of the bearded old man who sits face on to the viewer at the table and looks up at Jesus – is a matter of dispute.

These two altar paintings made Caravaggio famous overnight in Rome. His name became the talk of the town and further public commissions soon followed. Yet circumstances proved increasingly more difficult than positive. Caravaggio's unconventional approach encountered frequent criticism on the grounds of a lack of decorum. In the case of the next great commission, from Tiberio Cerasi on 24 September 1600, for two pictures for the Cerasi Chapel in S. Maria del Popolo,

Caravaggio's Working Method – The lack of surviving preparatory drawings has given rise to divided opinions among scholars. One view is that the artist generally did not make drawings, and revolutionised painting methods of his day by getting down his subjects directly on to the canvas *alla prima*, i.e. drawing inspiration from the sitter or from arranged groups of models. The other view is that there were indeed lots of drawings but these were destroyed or have been lost. As the greater part of Caravaggio's pictures are fully developed even at a preliminary stage, the latter view suggests that the basic compositional problems were solved not during the painting process but beforehand in the medium of drawing.

the first version of both pictures (*The Conversion of St Paul* and *The Martyrdom of St Peter*) was rejected and the painter had to supply revised versions. As recounted in the Bible, Saul the persecutor of Christians became Paul the Apostle after seeing a vision of Christ on the road to Damascus and being thrown to the ground. In his first version, Caravaggio had supplied an updated scene with a

One painting was rejected and a new version demanded

The Conversion of St Paul (1600/01), oil on wood, 237 × 189 cm, Private collection, Rome

The Conversion of St Paul (1600/01), oil on canvas, 230 × 175 cm, S. Maria del Popolo, Rome

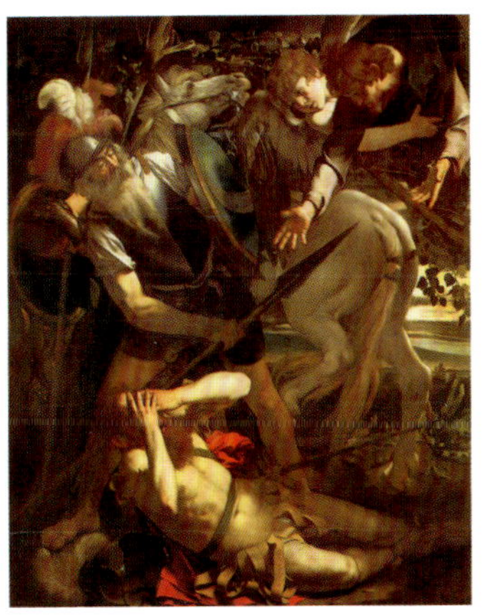

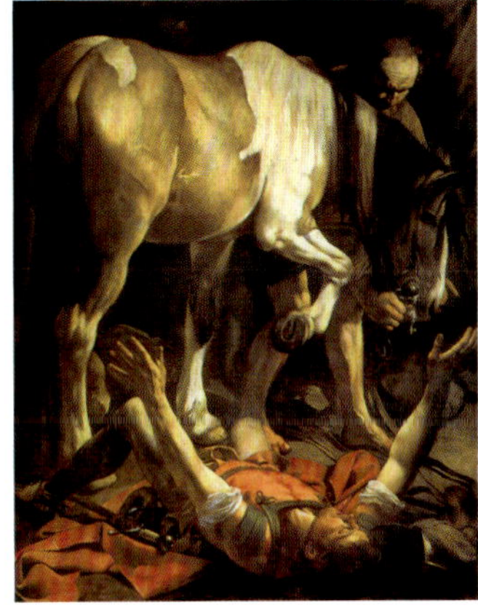

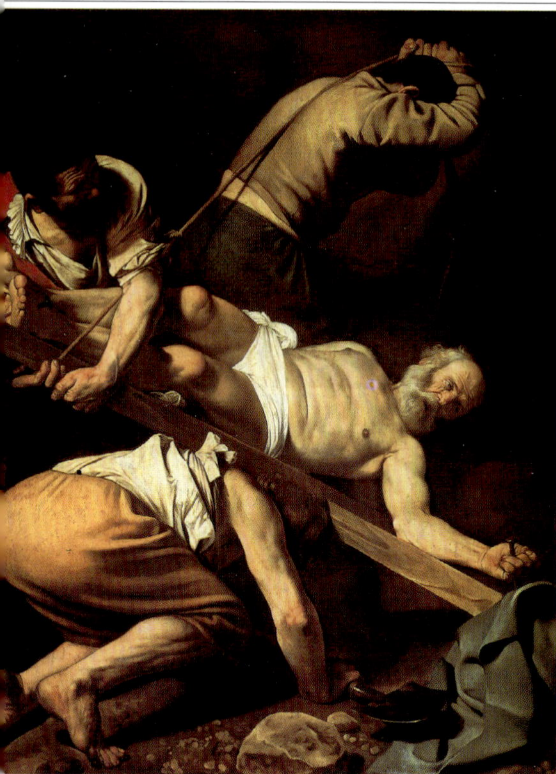

The Crucifixion of St Peter (1600/01), oil on canvas, 230 × 175 cm, S. Maria del Popolo, Rome

group of four people and a horse that was very difficult for the viewer to interpret. Saul, the intended convertee, appears faceless, holding both hands to his eyes in an effort to protect them from the brilliant light. Moreover, his leather-armoured body is distorted by his fall and makes him look as if posing, which would be unworthy of a saint. In the new version, Caravaggio reduced the event to two people plus the indispensable horse, which was essential for the conversion. This time Saul's face is visible, and both the older fellow traveller and the horse react visibly to the miracle.

In the other picture, the *Crucifixion of St Peter*, Caravaggio again limited the scene to just a few figures who occupy the whole pictorial frame. Three assistant executioners are seen erecting the cross with

Peter nailed to it. The scene suggests a penal execution, with no references to martyrdom at all. Against the dark background, the figures acquire an unusual sculptural quality from the hard light shining on them.

A work that was greeted with both admiration and criticism by contemporaries was *The Death of the Virgin*, for which Caravaggio signed a contract with the notary Laerzio Cherubini on 14 June 1601. This was destined for the family chapel of the Cherubinis in S. Maria della Scala. Here, too, the artist set the scene with the death of the Virgin in deep darkness, as an expression of grief. The gestures of the distressed apostles suggest shock and pain. Mary herself is lying on a pronouncedly shortened bed, her bodice undone, her skin greenish and her face puffy, while her bare feet reveal her soiled soles. Her countenance has no trace of the beautiful queen of heaven. As Baglione

The Virgin Mary is shown with soiled feet

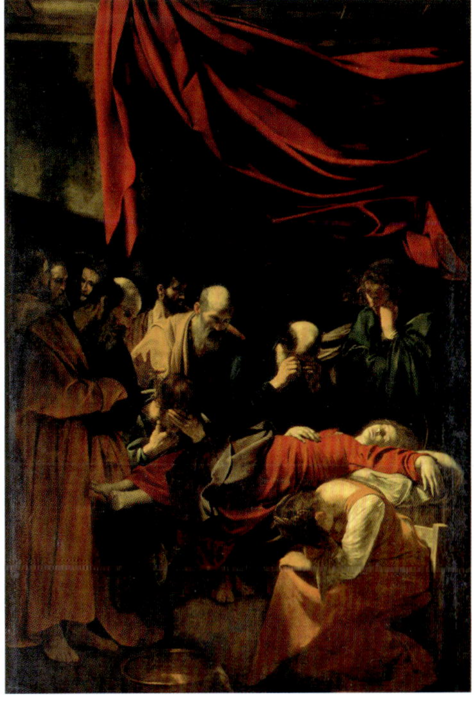

The Death of the Virgin (*c.* 1603), oil on canvas, 369 × 245 cm, Louvre, Paris

Angels guide the saint's hand

St Matthew and the Angel (1602), oil on canvas, 223 × 183 cm, destroyed, formerly Kaiser Friedrich Museum, Berlin

St Matthew and the Angel (1602/03), oil on canvas, 295 × 195 cm, S. Luigi dei Francesi, Rome

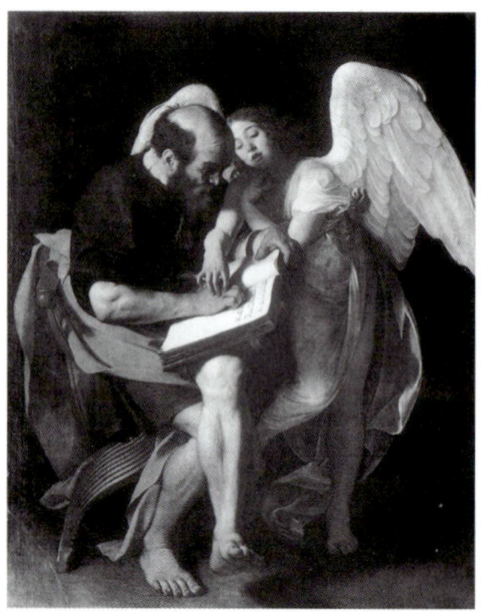

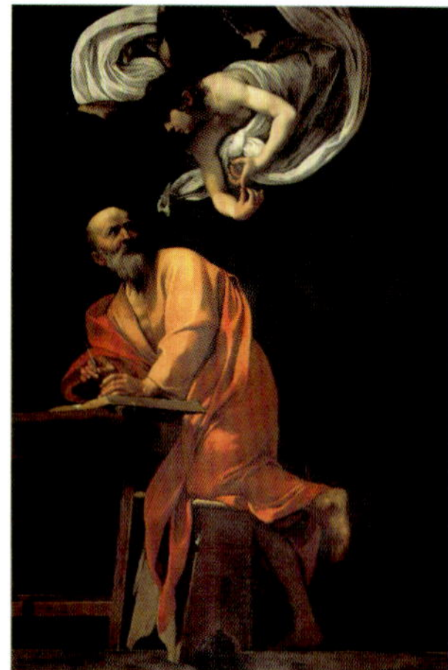

gleefully reports, the Discalced Carmelites ordered the painting to be removed from the church. On the advice of Peter Paul Rubens, the Duke of Mantua subsequently acquired it in 1607, though before it was removed, it was exhibited for a week in Rome at the request of artist colleagues of Caravaggio, who was in Malta at the time.

In 1602, Caravaggio received a further commission for the Contarelli chapel, for which he had already supplied two paintings. Once again it was for a picture of St Matthew, this time writing his gospel with angelic assistance. Here too there were difficulties with the painting – complaints were made about the figure of the saint which was deemed vulgar, and the physical proximity of Matthew to the angel guiding his hand. The rejected version was bought by the Marchese Vincenzo Giustiniani.

In the revised version, the angel and the saint are kept apart in separate zones of the picture. St Matthew looks up at the angel, who conveys the correct words with hand and speech.

Caravaggio as a storyteller _ After moving out of Cardinal del Monte's household, Caravaggio initially lived in Cardinal Gerolamo Mattei's palazzo. In the following five years he kept changing domicile, living for a time as a sub-tenant in the Campo Marzio, then moving in with fellow artists again. The difficulties that his patrons had with his interpretations of Biblical themes do not seem in the least to have had the effect of leaving him without any commissions. In the following few years he had plenty to do and, even if a version of a painting proved unwelcome to the original client, it did not take long for another purchaser to snap it up.

The basket of fruit appears again as a still-life motif

The Supper at Emmaus (1601), oil on canvas, 141 × 196.2 cm, National Gallery, London

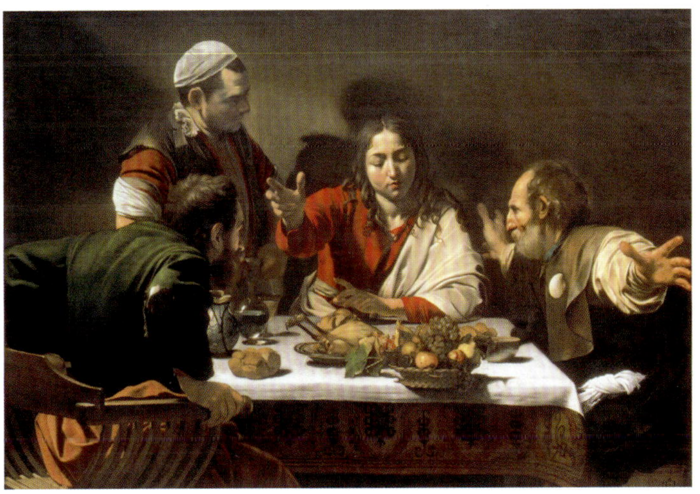

For the Marchese Ciriaco Mattei, Caravaggio painted *The Supper at Emmaus*. The story is again taken from the Bible, where two disciples leave Jerusalem for Emmaus on Easter Monday and meet up with another traveller on the way. Only when the stranger breaks bread at the meal in the inn do they recognise him as the Risen Christ. The amazement of the two disciples is reflected in dramatic gestures: one spreads his hands in astonishment, the other is so surprised he jumps up from his seat. Caravaggio included several still life motifs in the painting. For example, the fruit basket familiar from previous works hangs off the front edge of the table, projecting a shadow in the shape of a fish – the Eucharistic symbol of Communion.

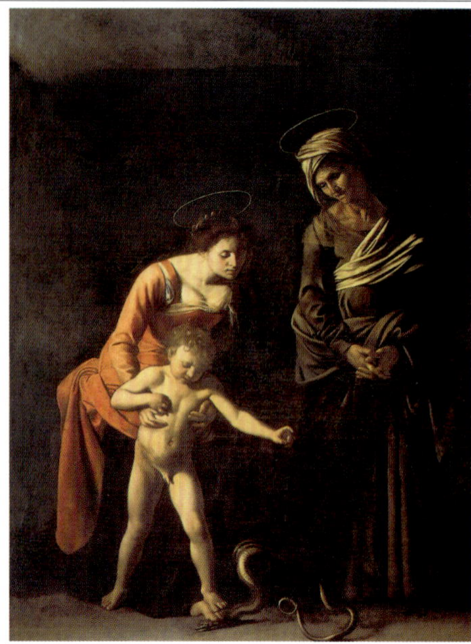

Madonna dei Palafrenieri
(1605/06), oil on canvas,
292 × 211 cm,
Galleria Borghese, Rome

Madonna dei Palafrenieri, which Caravaggio painted in 1605 at the behest of the Fraternity of S. Ana di Palafrenieri ('Masters of the Papal Horse') for their altar in St Peter's, also encountered criticism. Mary looked like a washerwoman in a dress and apron, it was said, and the Child was shown in all his nakedness. Finally, St Anne was described as looking like a peasant from somewhere near Rome. Hung in March 1606, barely a month later the painting was taken down again and sold to Cardinal Scipione Borghese.

For the *Madonna dei Pellegrini*, painted for the monks of Sant'-Agostino in 1606, the model was Lena, mentioned in the documents as the 'donna di Caravaggio'. She had previously posed for the Palafrenieri painting. Once again, Caravaggio strays from the usual iconography, where the Loreto madonnas appears in a heavenly zone over the altar area while the pilgrims kneel before an altar. Here, Mary leans humbly against a door frame like a peasant and accepts the respectful greetings of a pair of pilgrims whose feet are covered with dust from the road.

The Mother of God as a human being

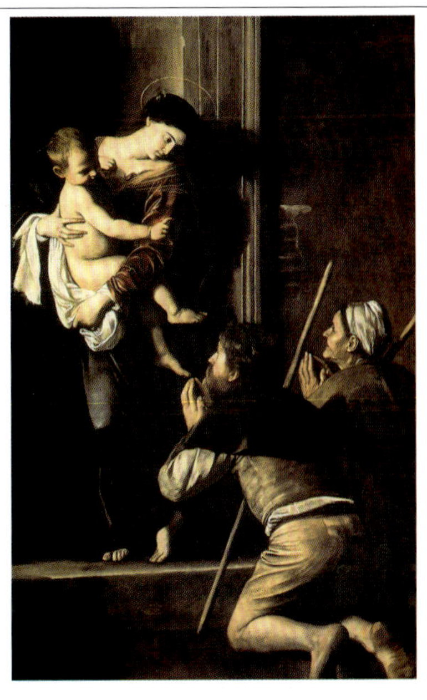

Madonna dei Pellegrini (1603–06), oil on canvas, 260 × 150 cm, S. Agostino, Rome

Deadly games _ Whereas Caravaggio had previously come off quite lightly in all the numerous brushes with the law over the previous six years, an incident in May 1606 had fatal consequences and would permanently change Caravaggio's life. On 28 May, following a game of *pallacorda* – a kind of rounders – a dispute broke out between the two teams of four players, one captained by Caravaggio, the other by Ranuccio Tomassoni from Terni. Each accused the other side of cheating. A fight broke out between Caravaggio and Tomassoni, during which weapons were drawn. Both men were wounded, but Tomassoni died of his wounds the following day. Caravaggio subsequently took to his heels and made for one of the estates of his patron Prince Mario Colonna in either Paliano, Zaragolo or Palestrina in the hills east of Rome. He was accused of murder and sentenced to death in his absence. In addition he was excommunicated, which meant that any member of the Corte could carry out the verdict in any place. He therefore had to take refuge somewhere outside the reach of Roman jurisdiction.

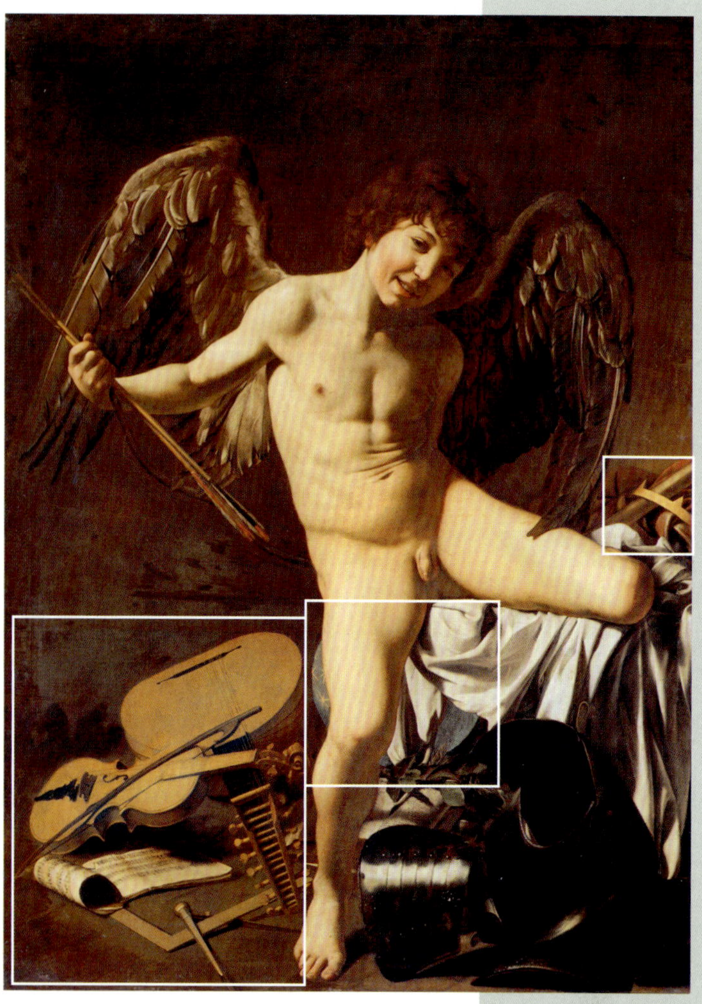

Victorious Cupid (Amor Vincit Omnia) (1602), oil on canvas, 191 × 148 cm, Gemäldegalerie, Staatliche Museen Preussischer Kulturbesitz, Berlin

Victorious Cupid

Amore vincente as the Amor of Vincens _ Caravaggio includes the client in the picture

Painted in 1602, *Victorious Cupid* may be one of Caravaggio's best-known pictures but, as the only explicitly allegorical work, it is at the same time untypical of his œuvre. He painted it in the course of his dispute with Giovanni Baglione. Both painters completed works for the Giustiniani Genoese banking family. Baglione was commissioned to paint *Celestial Love* for Cardinal Benedetto Giustiniani, while Caravaggio did the counterpart *Victorious Cupid* for the cardinal's secular brother Vincenzo. The banker proudly paid 300 scudi for his picture – the price of a large altar painting. The differing choice of subject matter matched of course the respective ecclesiasitical and profane statuses of the brothers. Whereas Caravaggio's work was greeted with great admiration, Baglione encountered only mockery with his. According to a report by the Netherlandish painter and art writer Joachim von Sandrart, who acted as curator of the gallery at the Palazzo Giustiniani from 1623 to 1635, *Victorious Cupid* constituted the conclusion and the climax of every tour and, to enhance the drama of its presentation, it was apparently hidden behind a curtain.

The scene is of a smiling boy about twelve years old, half seated on a table and on the point of climbing over a series of objects. With wings spread and a bow and pair of arrows in his right hand, he is unmistakable as Cupid, the god of Love. Caravaggio's treatment of the naked body here is particularly free and notable in allowing a view of the boy's sex. At Cupid's feet are several musical instruments, a violin and a lute, an open book of music, weapons, a shield and a globe of the night sky. On his right are a crown, a general's baton and purple fabric. *Prima facie* the painting is to be interpreted as showing the victory of carnal love over all values, on the strength of Virgil's plattitude: *amor vincit omnia*. Yet the picture is also allusively structured and designed to bear the imprint of the client as well. Thus the objects on show have been taken as allusions to Vincenzo Giustiniani's own praiseworthy characteristics. Musical instruments and sheet music refer to the client's

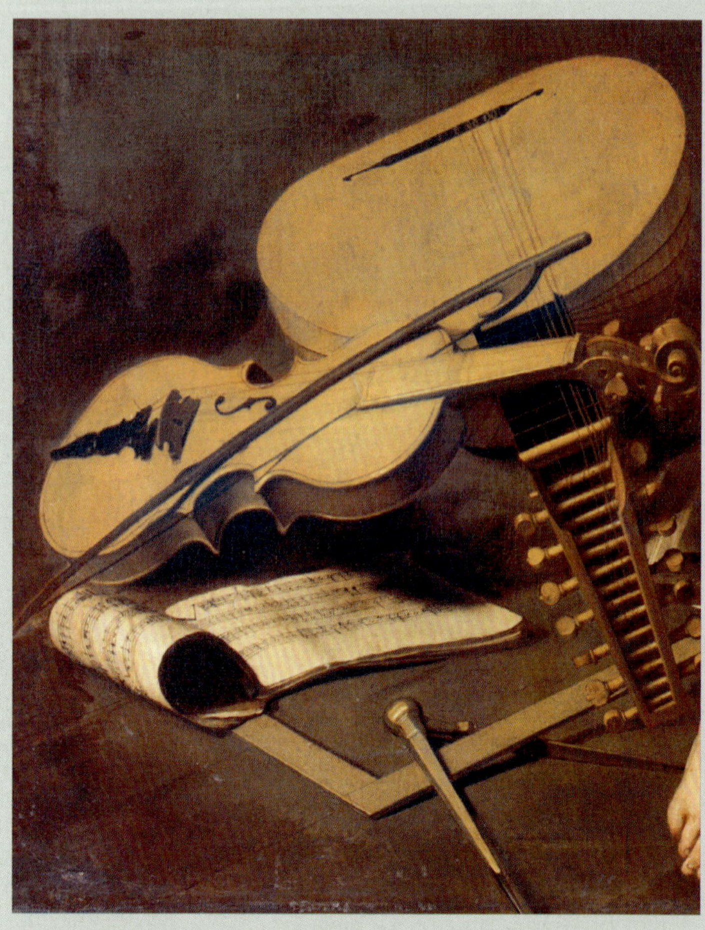

skills as an active amateur musician and music lover. The globe is also a symbol of music here, alluding to the music of the spheres. Set square and compasses are normally attributes of geometry and mathematics, but are also the tools of the architect. This is therefore an allusion to Giustiniani's knowledge of architecture and architectural theory – he had directed the work of rebuilding his palazzo in the little town of Bassano di Sutri and had also written an architectural treatise. The weapons and the propped up metal shield are references to Vincezo's military prowess. Whereas the above objects all lie at Cupid's feet in the painting, the crown, commander's baton and purple fabric are

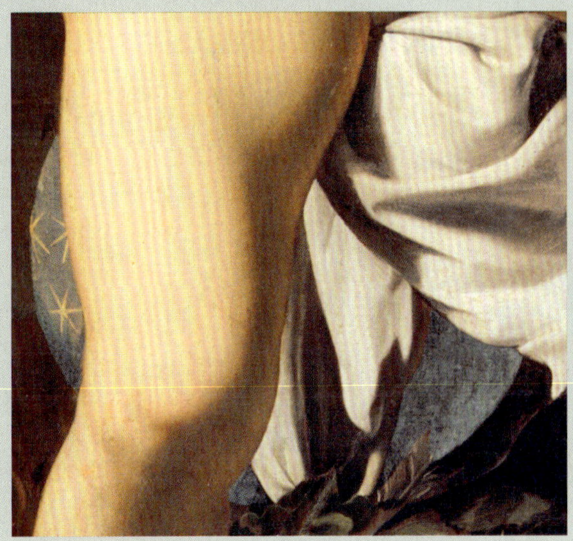

alongside him, at the same height. This is a reference to the princely, almost royal rank of the Giustiniani family, whose made-up family geneology traces them back to the Emperor Justinian.

There are also quite specific allusions to the client's first name in the picture. For example, the metal set square forms a V-shaped motif, which is taken to refer to Vincenzo. An open pair of compasses is hidden in the set square in such a way that it could constitute an A. In the context of Virgil's literary bromide *amor vincit omnia*, the viewer is prompted to see the victorious Cupid (*amore vincente* or *amor vincens*) in the picture as specifically as the name Vincens. Thanks to the simple parallel, the *Amore Vincente* can be seen in the context of the collection as an *Amor* of Vincens, and thus bearing the owner's name.

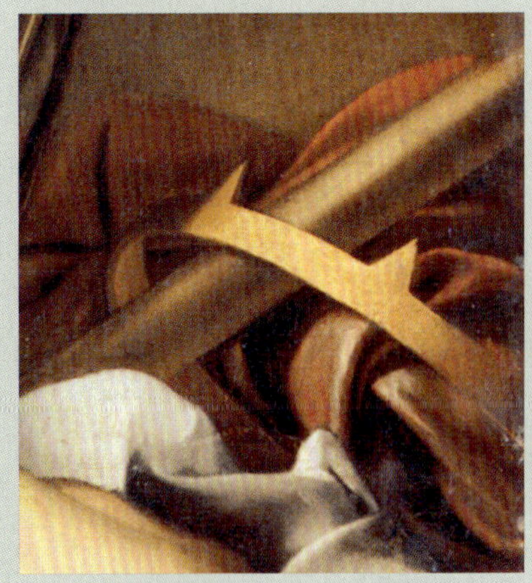

1606–1610

On the Run and a Return to Naples

Success in Naples _ With the Knights of St John _ The year in Sicily _ Stop-off in Naples _ Death in Porto Ercole

Though the previous six years in Rome had been turbulent enough, what with incidents and conflicts with the authorities and the constant threat of legal action, court hearings and spells in prison, Caravaggio spent the last four years of his life even less comfortably, mostly on the run. The astonishing thing is that, despite such a background of instability, this period remained one of enormous productivity. He supplied numerous monumental altar paintings and a whole series of paintings for private picture galleries on mainly religious topics. Among his patrons in the last years of his life were the Spanish Viceroy, religious orders, the aristocrats of Naples, Malta and Sicily and the Senate of Messina.

Success in Naples _ Caravaggio fled the death sentence in Rome to Naples, where he remained less than two years from the end of September 1606. His fame in Rome had preceded him and, when he reached Naples, clients were waiting who were not interested in his criminal record. Caravaggio's effect on Neapolitan painting is much stronger than his influence on painting in Rome. Despite his relatively short stay of around eighteen months, the quantity of works he completed in that time was very large. The number of panel paintings suggest that the artist committed his subject matter to canvas with incredible speed. His inspiration was sufficiently forceful for the artists in Naples to finally abandon the traditions of the late sixteenth century. Thus Caravaggio's influence on Neapolitan painting was powerful and long-lasting.

Caravaggio completed the monumental *Seven Works of Mercy*, commissioned by the Congregazione del Monte Pio della Misericordia for the main altar of their church, by January 1607. The picture depicts a Madonna and Child floating on a cloud looking down on seven acts of

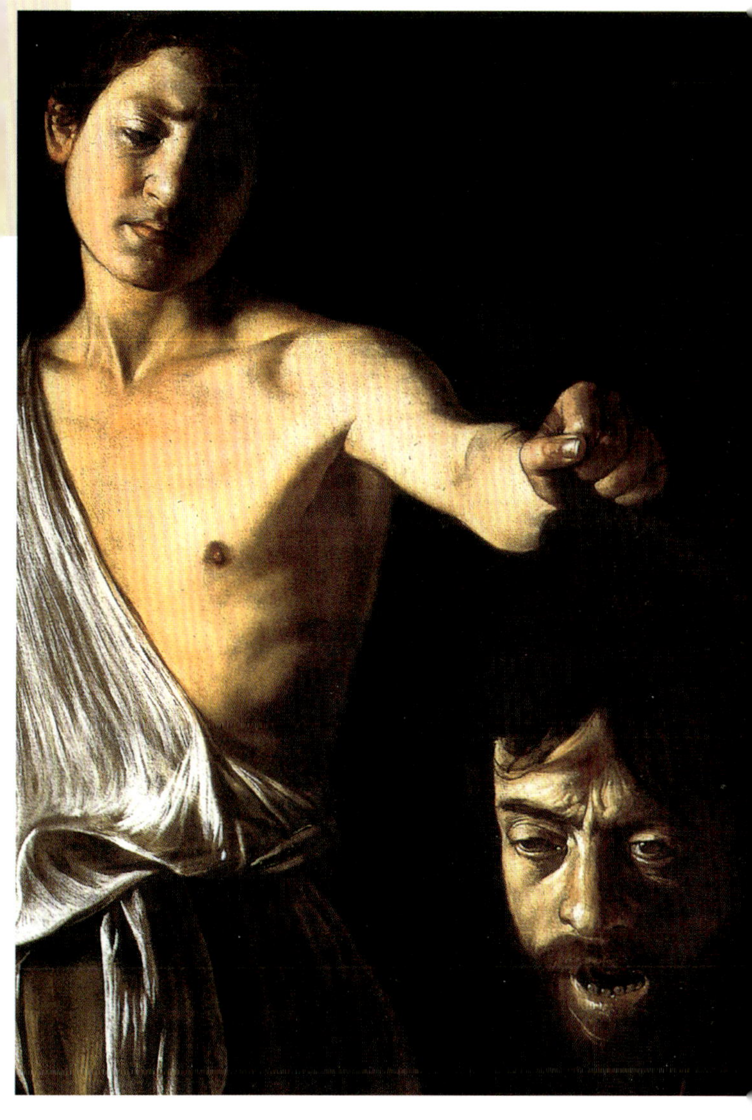

Goliath's head bears Caravaggio's features

David with the Head of Goliath (1610), detail, oil on canvas, 125 × 101 cm, Galleria Borghese, Rome

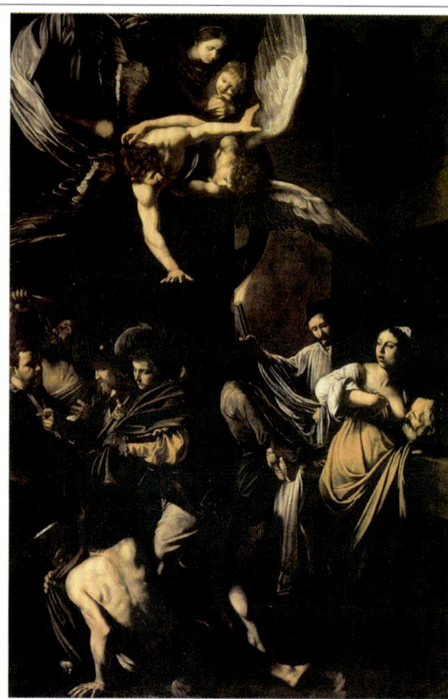

The Seven Works of Mercy (1606/07), oil on canvas, 390 × 260 cm, Pio Monte della Misericordia, Naples

mercy. A number of figures from various periods have gathered outside a building whose barred windows show it is a prison, and are doing good deeds. A publican is giving accommodation to the Apostle James, on the left Samson is receiving a drink thanks to a miracle and, in the foreground, St Martin is in the process of sharing his cloak with a freezing, naked man. The young woman on the right feeding a prisoner alludes to a *caritas romana* motif.

Who originally commissioned the altar painting of *The Madonna of the Rosary*, which turned up on the Neapolitan art market in September 1607, is not known, but it was bought by Vincenzo I Gonzaga, Duke of Mantua. Similarities in the features of the client shown at the bottom on the left suggest it was Count of Benavente, the Viceroy of Naples. The scene is of the Virgin appearing to St Dominic and handing him the rosary. She taught him to pray with it and instructed him to popularise it for devotions. Caravaggio dispenses with the usual hierarchical division into two scenes of a heavenly and an earthly zone,

St Dominic interceding with the Madonna for the populace

The Madonna of the Rosary (1606/07), oil on canvas, 364.5 × 249.5 cm, Kunsthistorisches Museum, Vienna

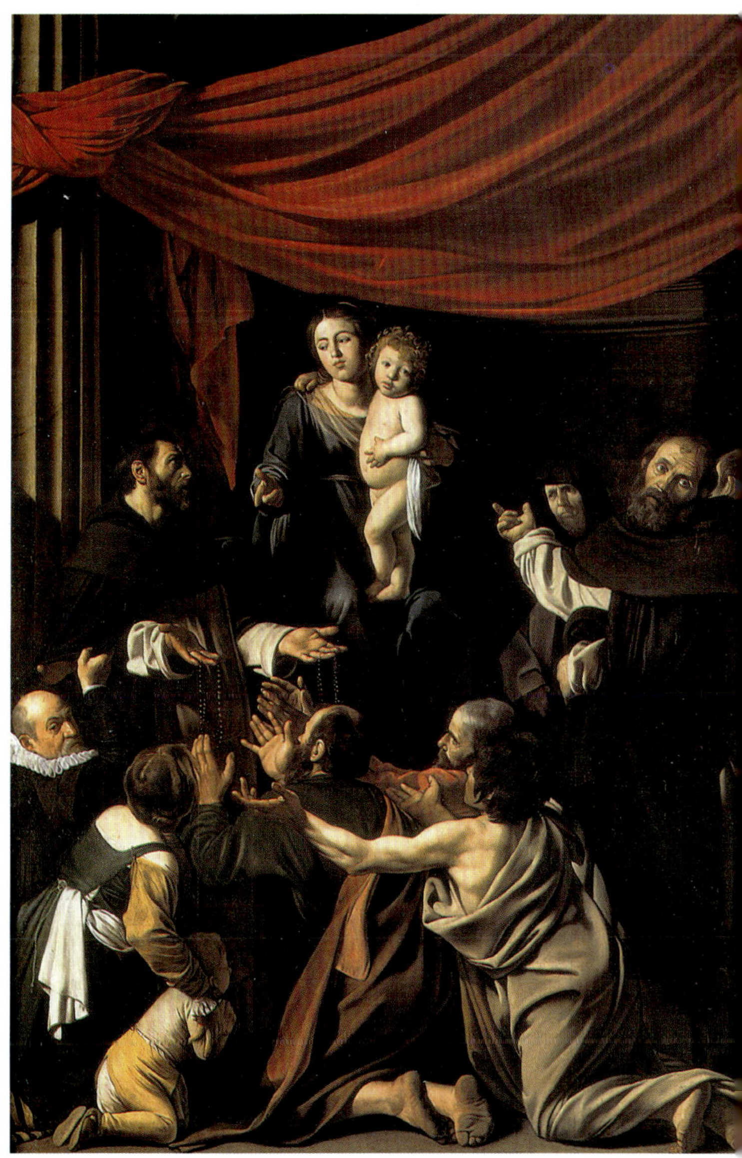

Christ as a portly, human figure

Flagellation (*c.* 1607), oil on canvas, 134.5 × 175.5 cm, Musée des Beaux-Arts, Rouen

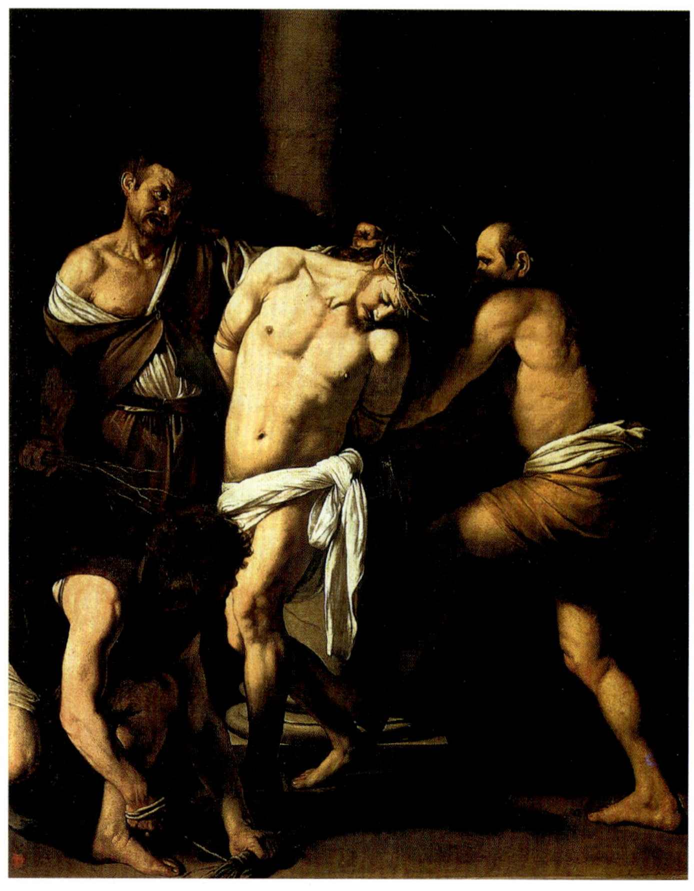

bringing all the figures together into a large group. Despite this, however, the painting displays the strict ecclesiastical hierarchy newly propagated by the Counter-Reformation, whereby ordinary people could have no direct access to the Virgin but required the intercession of the saints.

In May 1607, Tommaso de Franchis commissioned the artists to paint a flagellation scene for the family chapel of the de Franchis in S. Domenico Maggiore. Caravaggio places the unclad Christ, an unusually full figure wearing the crown of thorns, in the centre of the painting. He is flanked by three ruffians – one has bound him, the one kneeling in front is tying a bundle of twigs together and the third is already laying into him. Whereas the figure of Christ stands virtually wholly in the light, the ruffians are half-absorbed by the darkness and are only partly visible. Unconventional features in Caravaggio's picture are not only the rather corpulent Christ but also the sheer brutality of the ruffians' treatment of him.

With the Knights of St John _ Why, despite all these commissions and successes, Caravaggio left Naples can only be guessed at. Baglione asserts that he was ambitious to be admitted to the Knights of St John in Malta. Possibly he hoped that, if he were accepted into the order, it would speed up his petition for a pardon from the Pope. In July 1607, he boarded a ship for the crossing to Malta and was in the capital Valletta by 13 July at the latest. His stay is Malta is poorly documented. Alof de Wignacourt, a Grand Master of the order, played an important part in efforts to get Caravaggio admitted to the order and probably passed on several commissions to him. The commission for an altar painting of the *Beheading of St John* for the oratory of the Cathedral of S. Giovanni dei Cavalieri also came from Wignacourt.

A stiff portrait of the Grand Master

Portrait of Alof de Wignacourt (1608), oil on canvas, 194 × 134 cm, Louvre, Paris

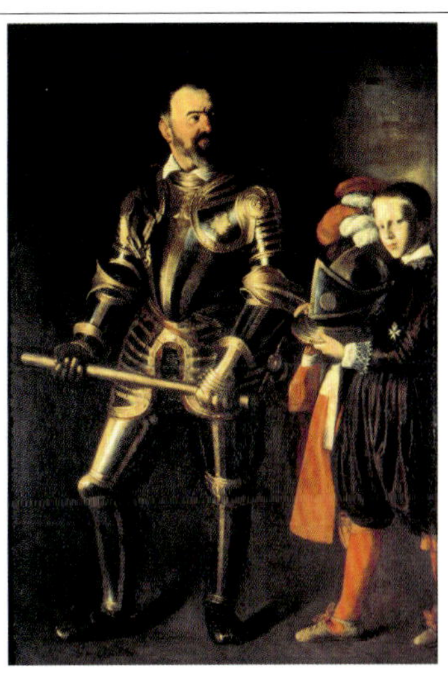

Sleeping Cupid (1608), oil on canvas, 71 × 105 cm, Palazzo Pitti, Florence

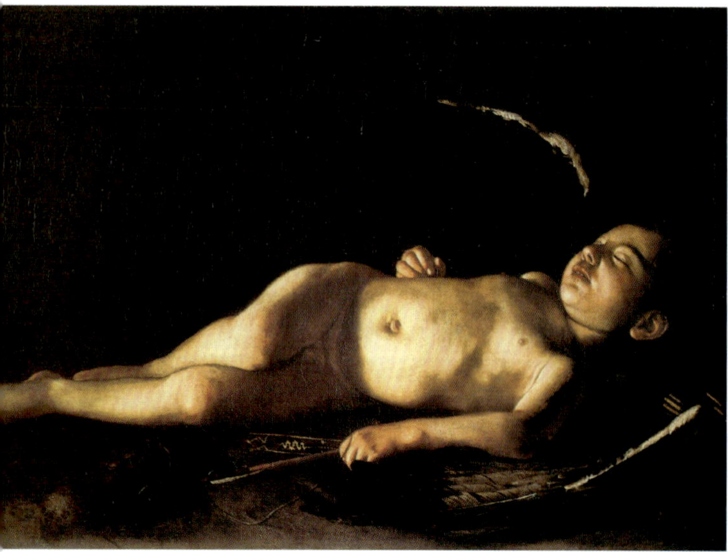

Even in Rome and later in Naples, Caravaggio had already done many portraits of the clerical and secular aristocracy and mercantile classes, though most of them have been lost. The large-format portrait of Alof de Wignacourt dated 1608 was commissioned by the subject himself. Against a dark, neutral background Caravaggio paints him as a full-length figure facing the viewer frontally, wearing armour and with his heavy commander's staff in his hand. On the right, a pretty page enters, bringing helmet and crest. The painting is reminiscent of Titian's full-length portraits but, in contrast with those, looks clumsy and stiff.

Sleeping Cupid, one of the few paintings with a mythological subject from Caravaggio's late period, likewise dates to the time in Malta. A comparison with the well-shaped boys and small children of the works from the artist's Roman period in the 1590s shows how much his attitude has changed. This Cupid is an ugly, tubby child whose puffy lower body and misformed chest suggest ill-health.

Despite the pull of Wignacourt and the artist's successes with his paintings, Caravaggio's admittance to the Maltese order did not go off

A funeral in a sombre atmosphere

The Burial of St Lucy (1608), oil on canvas, 408 × 300 cm, Museo di Palazzo Bellomo, Syracuse

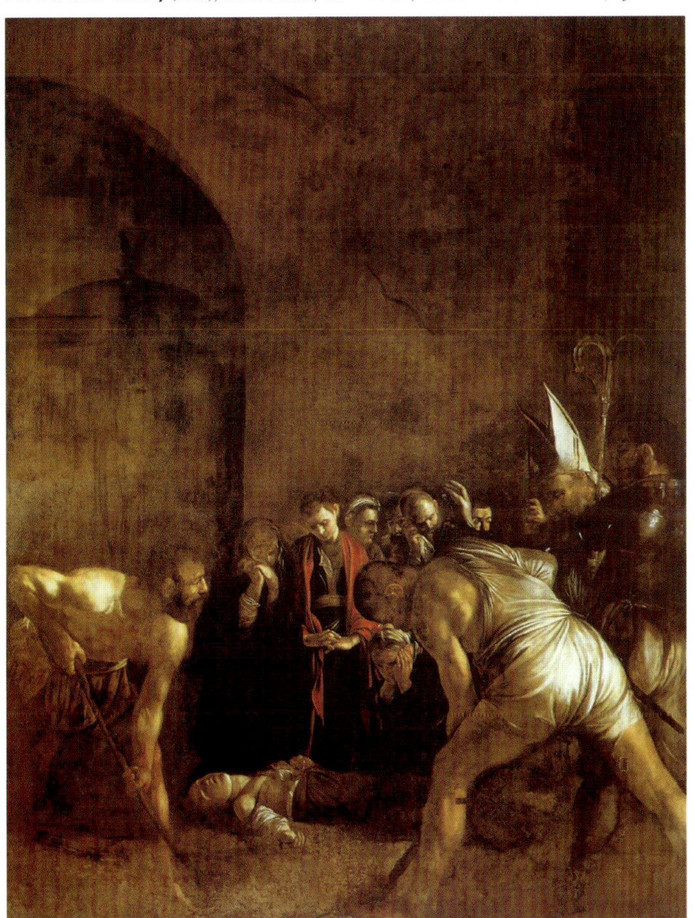

particularly smoothly. It appears from letters that the Grand Master wrote to the order's ambassador in Rome during this period that permission had been sought from the Pope to authorise the admittance of an unnamed person who had committed murder in a quarrel. This person not mentioned by name is in all probability Caravaggio. This indicates that the Knights of St John were aware of his criminal record. The Pope's dispensation arrived on 15 February 1608 and, on 14 July,

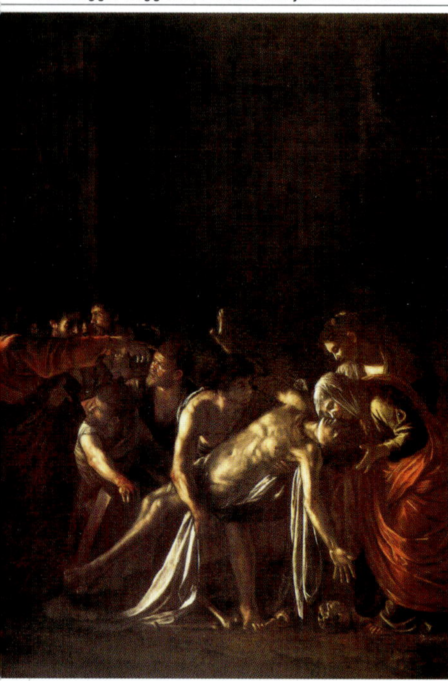

Raising of Lazarus (1608/09), oil on canvas, 380 × 275 cm, Museo Regionale, Messina

a year and a day after his arrival in Malta, the artist was admitted to the order. It was a rule that candidates had to spend at least one year in the monastery. Shortly after his admission, Caravaggio become involved in yet another quarrel. He was accused of having insulted a 'Cavaliere di Giustizia' and arrested. On 6 October, he escaped from the dungeon in the fort of S. Angelo and set sail for Sicily. This latest conflict with the law resulted in the painter being excluded from the order, a decision taken on 20 November 1608 and put into force on 1 December.

The year in Sicily _ Caravaggio spent almost a year in Sicily, from October 1608. After a few months in Syracuse he went on to Messina and finally reached Palermo. The feverish restlessness of these months has given rise to the assumption that the painter was always on the run for fear of possible acts of reprisal. However, whatever his personal situation may have been, he painted several masterpieces in each of these cities that reaped him great recognition. He had hardly arrived in Syracuse – it is assumed he went there at the suggestion of a painter friend, Mario Minniti, whom he knew from Rome and who also took him in – when he immediately won a commission for an altar painting. In winter 1608, the senate of the City of Syracuse ordered from Caravaggio a painting on the subject of the burial of St Lucy for the church of S. Lucia. The dead woman is placed on the ground in a dark, dreary vaulted room. She is surrounded by a bishop, who blesses her, and the mourning congregation. In the foreground are two grave-diggers. The dark hollow eyes of the deceased allude to her martyrdom when her eyes were torn out.

On 10 July 1609, we find Caravaggio in Messina, where he worked on a painting for the Genoese merchant Giovan Battista de' Lazzari, destined for the Cappella Lazzari in the Crusader church. At the painter's suggestion, the subject originally planned – a Madonna with St John the Baptist and other saints – was changed to the *Raising of Lazarus*, in allusion to the client's family name. The scene is shrouded in deep darkness into which not even the figure of Christ brings light as he comes to awaken Lazarus. Lazarus appears here as a real corpse already in a state of decay.

Downcast David

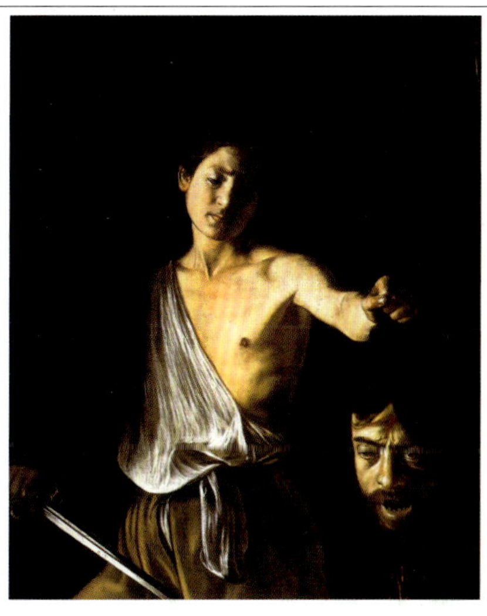

David with the Head of Goliath (*c.* 1610), oil on canvas, 125 × 101 cm, Galleria Borghese, Rome

The genesis of *David with the Head of Goliath* is also dated to the time in Sicily. Caravaggio shows David here as a melancholy hero, looking at the severed head with down-cast expression. It is seen by some as an ironic allusion to his own troubles that Goliath, known in Jewish tradition as the 'dirty whore-son', bears the painter's own features.

Stop-off in Naples _ On 24 October 1609, Caravaggio was at work in Naples again and once more involved in a brawl. This time he was attacked in the *osteria* of the Cerriglios and sustained a cut in the face. Baglione describes it as an act of revenge. During the months in Naples he again painted numerous works, some of which have disappeared, such as the altar panels for the Cappella Fenaroli in S. Anna dei Lombardi. His last documented painting depicts another martyrdom, a subject he kept returning to throughout his career. In this case it is *The Martyrdom of St Ursula*, a commission from the Genoese

Spanish Naples _ From 1516 to 1700, Naples along with Sicily and Malta belonged to the empire of the Spanish Habsburgs, and the three were ruled by a viceroy based in Naples. During the Renaissance, the latter was of little importance as a centre of art, but in the seventeenth century it became not only one of the leading cultural and commercial centres of Europe but also one of the most important Mediterranean ports. For artists, it was an excellent place to seek commissions. Apart from the Spanish viceroy, the aristocracy, members of religious orders and prosperous merchants lived amid the trappings of ostentation and splendour and had palazzos, piazzas and churches newly built and fitted out.

prince Marcantonio Doria, who paid for it in May 1610 and had it shipped to Genoa. The scene depicts Ursula being murdered by the heathen king of the Huns, whose advances she had spurned. Remarkably, all those present radiate melancholy. Caravaggio's depiction of the Hunnish king with bow at the ready is interpreted as a deliberate 'error' by the painter – the arrow in the bow is intended for Ursula, who stands beside him.

Death in Porto Ercole _ The circumstances of Caravaggio's death remain somewhat obscure. In July 1610 he boarded a felucca, taking some paintings with him in his baggage. He was heading for Rome, where Cardinal Gonzaga was endeavouring to get him a pardon. The felucca was seized in Palo, where Caravaggio was arrested, probably as a result of mistaken identity. It is conjectured that his pursuers may

A conscious 'error' in the picture

The Martyrdom of St Ursula (1610), oil on canvas, 154 × 178 cm, Banca Commerciale Italiana, Naples

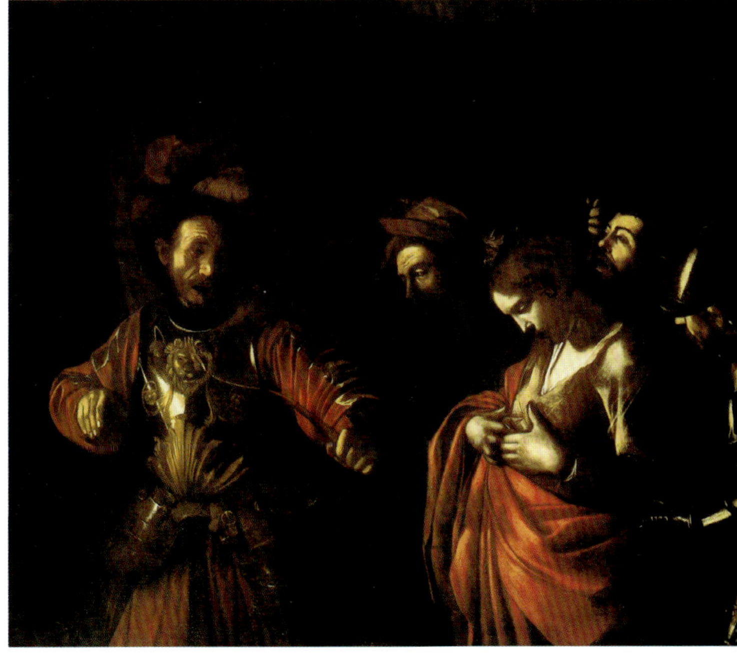

have had a hand in this, as he had been constantly on the run from them in Sicily. After two days in prison he was released on bail for a substantial sum. Caravaggio attempted to reach the boat, which of course had returned to Naples with the pictures. He continued his journey to Rome on foot, but died of fever on the way in Porto Ercole, on 18 July. Baglione's gloss was that Caravaggio died "as wretchedly as he lived."

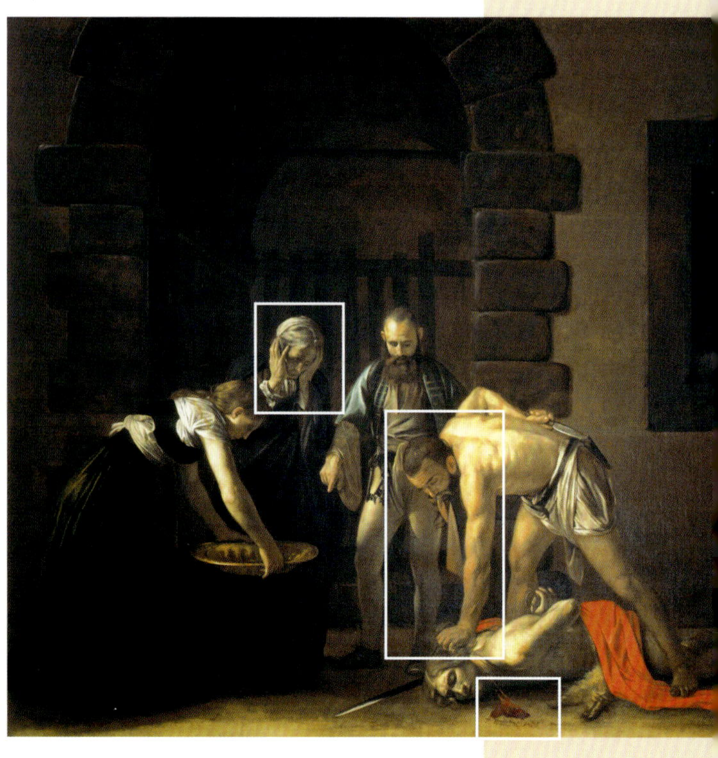

The Beheading of St John the Baptist (1608), oil on canvas, 361 × 520 cm, S. Giovanni, Valletta

The Beheading of St John the Baptist

A sombre mood affects all present – Caravaggio as the creator of modern tragedy in painting

Caravaggio painted this monumental painting during his stay in Malta, where he had fled to from Naples in summer 1607. It is the artist's largest painting, surpassing even the formats of the Roman altar paintings. He soon proved very successful in Malta as well, which prompted the Grand Master of the Knights of St John, Alof de Wignacourt, to commission a painting from him on the subject of the beheading of John the Baptist. It was intended for the oratory of the cathedral of S. Giovanni dei Cavalieri in Valletta.

As the Gospels report, John the Baptist was imprisoned by Herod Antipas after John had accused the king of unlawful union with his sister-in-law Herodias. Filled with spite, Herodias prevailed on her daughter Salome to demand the head of John after her father, seduced by her dancing, had granted her a wish. John was duly beheaded and Salome presented the head to her mother on a platter.

Caravaggio shifted the scene to a prison courtyard. In the middle, the dead John the Baptist lies on the ground with staring eyes. Blood spurts from his neck and his hands are tied behind his back. A red cloth and a piece of fur pelt cover his buttocks. The executioner is bent over him, having put down his sword after delivering the blow, and is about to hack off the head with a dagger. Beside him stands a man whom the key in his belt marks out as a jailer, urging the executioner to place the head on a bowl, which Salome leans forward to hold out to him. Beside

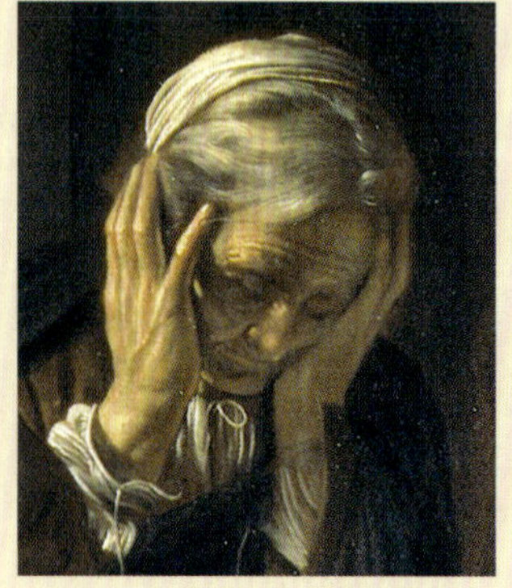

her, an old woman claps her hands over her face. Two other mute witnesses are prisoners following events through the bars of their cells.

The scene completely lacks the drama that Caravaggio had created in the *Martyrdom of St Matthew*. Here the painter concentrates the scene on essentials, reducing the action to just a few figures acting in a dark, large, rather empty space. The participants are brought out of the darkness by sharp light, with only John and the executioner being completely illuminated. In the *Beheading of St John* we have an executioner who is far from triumphant. The physicality of the figures is also muted. They do not have the occasionally brutal-looking massiveness of other scenes of martyrdom. The whole group around the dead John seems in fact struck dumb with horror. Salome holds the bowl in a pose of stillness, without overt emotion, the attitude of the old woman indicates silent distress, the gestures of the jailer are restrained, and the two prisoners watch the execution in a trance. They are all absorbed in the event depicted, each of them apparently overcome by grief and dismay which freezes them in monumental stillness.

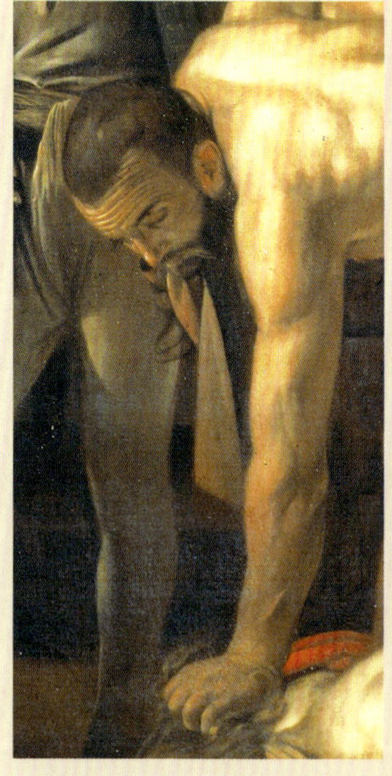

The painting occupies a special position in the artist's œuvre in that it is the only surviving work he signed. The signature is *F Michel A*, written with the blood of the murdered prophet. The *A* stands for 'Angelo', the *F* could be *Fra* (i.e. a knight of the Order of St John) or *fecit* (painted by).

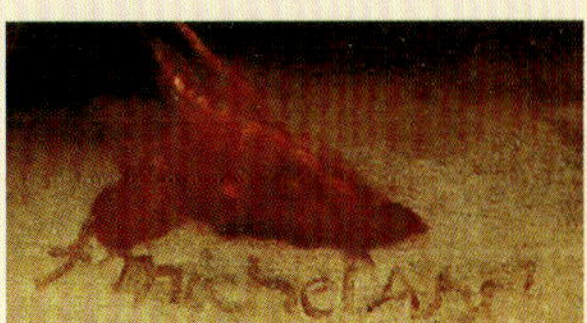
Detail of the artist's signature

Caravaggio returned to the subject of St John the Baptist many times throughout his life. In most paintings, the saint is seen sitting in the woods or the desert, sometimes with a lamb or ram at his side. With these pictures of St John, who has left the city and seeks solitude for atonement or meditation, he established an enduring type for the youthful saint. The beheading was a subject that was favoured in the Catholic south, whereas in the north the subject of St John preaching tended to be chosen. The Catholic Church preferred a picture of a saint sacrificing himself, ready for the ultimate act, to the Baptist acting autonomously, preaching or performing miracles. Caravaggio's monumental painting, which today is considered the first modern tragedy in painting, drew numerous travellers to Malta to admire it.

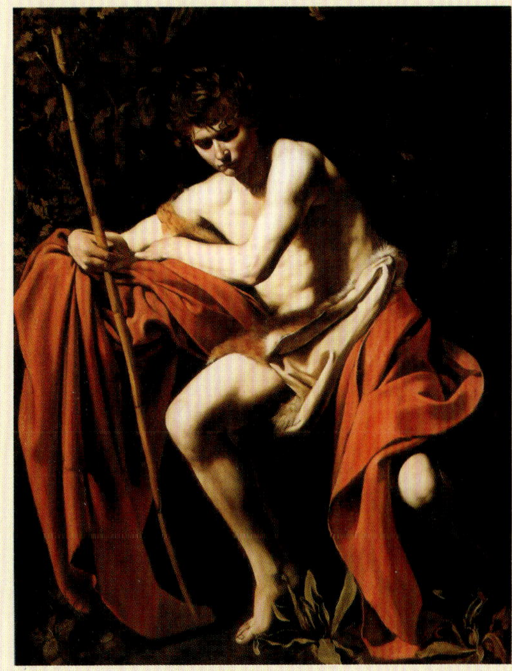
St John the Baptist (1603–1605), oil on canvas, 173.4 × 132.1 cm Nelson-Atkins Museum of Art, Kansas City

Where can Caravaggios's works be seen?

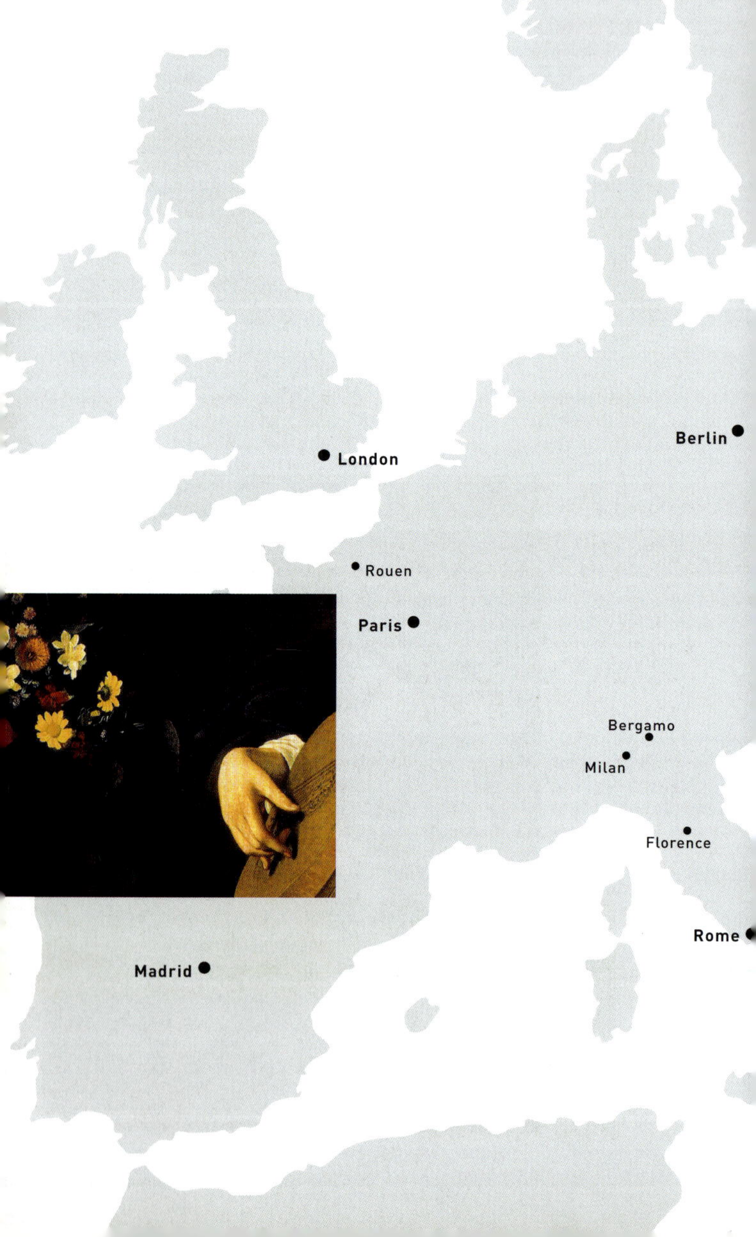

London
Berlin
Rouen
Paris
Bergamo
Milan
Florence
Rome
Madrid

St Petersburg

North America

Toronto

Cleveland

Hartford

Kansas

New York

San Francisco

Los Angeles

Fort Worth

Vienna

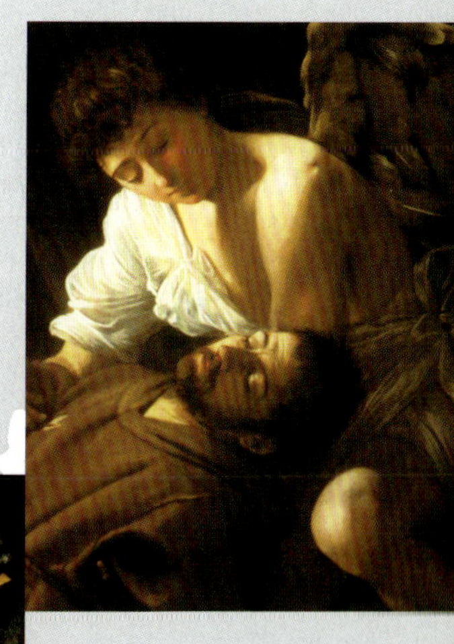

Naples

Messina

Syracuse

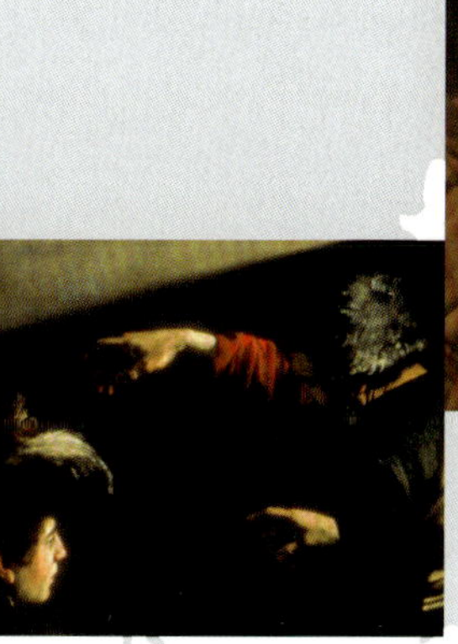

A selection of museums housing some of Caravaggio's most famous works:

- **Bergamo**
  Accademia Carrara
  Piazza Carrara 82/a
  www.accademiacarrara.bergamo.it

- **Berlin**
  Staatliche Museen zu Berlin – Preußischer Kulturbesitz
  Gemäldegalerie Kulturforum
  Matthäikirchplatz 4
  www.smb.spk-berlin.de

- **Cleveland**, Ohio
  The Cleveland Museum of Art
  11150 East Boulevard
  www.clevelandart.org

- **Florence**
  Galleria degli Uffizi
  Piazale degli Uffizi 6
  www.musa.uffizi.firenze.it

  Palazzo Pitti
  Piazzi Pitti 1
  www.sbas.firenze.it/musei/pitti2. html

- **Fort Worth**
  Kimbell Art Museum
  3333 Camp Bowie Boulevard
  www.kimbellart.org

- **Hartford**
  Wadsworth Atheneum
  600 Main Street
  www.wadsworthatheneum.org

- **Kansas**
  The Nelson Atkins Museum of Art
  4525 Oak Street
  www.nelson-atkins.org

- **London**
  National Gallery
  Trafalgar Square
  www.nationalgallery.org.uk

- **Los Angeles**
  The Getty Center
  1200 Getty Center Drive
  www.getty.edu

- **Madrid**
  Museo Nacional del Prado
  Paseo del Prado
  www.museoprado.es

  Museo Thyssen-Bornemisza
  Paseo del Prado 8
  www.museothyssen.org

- **Messina**
  Museo Regionale
  Via della Libertà 465

- **Milan**
  Pinacoteca di Brera
  Via Brera 28
  www.brera.beniculturali.it
  Pinacoteca Ambrosiana
  Piazza Pio XI 2
  www.ambrosiana.it

- **Naples**
  Museo di Capodimonte
  Via Milano 1

New York
The Metropolitan Museum of Art
1000 Fifth Avenue
www.metmuseum.org

Paris
Musée du Louvre
34–36, Quai du Louvre
www.louvre.fr

Rome
Galleria Borghese
Piazzale Scipione Borghese 5
www.galleriaborghese.it

Galleria Doria Pamphilj
Piazza del Collegio Romano 2
www.doriapamphilj.it

Galleria Nazionale d'Arte Antica
Palazzo Corsini
Via della Lungara 10
www.galleriaborghese.it/corsini

Vatican Museums
Vatican City
mv.vatican.va

Rouen
Musée des Beaux-Arts
Esplanade Marcel Duchamp

San Francisco
Fine Arts Museums of
San Francisco
34th Avenue and Clement Street
www.thinker.org

St Petersburg
State Hermitage
www.hermitagemuseum.org

Syracuse
Galleria regionale di
Palazzo Bellomo
Via G.M. Capodieci 14–16

Toronto, Ontario
Art Gallery of Ontario
317 Dundas Street West
www.ago.net

Vienna
Kunsthistorisches Museum
Burgring 5
www.khm.at

More about Caravaggio: a selection of books on the artist and his work

Caravaggio attracted the interest of art historians much later than other Baroque painters, despite his tremendous influence on contemporaries and subsequent generations of artists. It is only really in the last half century that the painter has become a centre of serious academic attention. Documentary findings in archives in Milan and Rome and newly attributed paintings have enabled art-historians to define with some accuracy which works really are by Caravaggio and to add and correct a number of biological dates. Although there are extensive references to the artist in secondary literature, a definitive catalogue raisonné of his works is still lacking.

Among publications giving an overview of Caravaggio's work and life and containing documents and vitae of contemporaries are a number of volumes that are now considered **standard academic works** such as Walter Friedländer's *Caravaggio Studies*, Princeton, N.J. 1955 and Roberto Longhi's *Caravaggio*, Dresden 1968. Several more recent publications are held in equally high regard, especially Howard Hibbard's *Caravaggio*, London 1983 (the most well-rounded, modern study available in English), Mia Cinotti, *Caravaggio, la vita e l'opera*, Bergamo 1991, Mina Gregori, *Caravaggio*, Milan 1994 and Catherine Publisi's well-illustrated *Caravaggio*, London, New York 1998.

The **most important biographies** and critical accounts are to be found in G. Mancini, *Considerazioni sulla pittura*, Rome *c.* 1617–30 (revised and edited by A. Marucchi and L. Salerno, in two volumes, Rome 1956–57), G. Baglione, *Vite*, 1642 (edited by V. Mariani in 1935), and G. P. Bellori, *Vite*, 1672 (edited by E. Borea in 1976). The most relevant passages from these works are reproduced in Howard Hibbard's definitive work mentioned above.

Much groundwork has also been covered in **exhibition catalogues** which include: *The Age of Caravaggio*, New York and Rome 1985, *Michelangelo Merisi da Caravaggio. Come nascono i capolavori*, Florence and Rome 1992 (edited by M. Gregori, this excellently illustrated volume includes an extensive discussion on Caravaggio's technique, as well as tackling questions of attribution including a summary of recent scholarship), and the exhibition catalogue *Caravaggio: The Last Years*, Naples and London 2004/05.

Straightforward **introductions** to the life and work of Caravaggio include Timothy Wilson-Smith, *Caravaggio*, London 1998, Rosa Giorgi, *Caravaggio: Master of Light and Dark – His Life in Paintings*, Cologne 1998, Helen Langdon, *Caravaggio: A Life*, New York 1999, Gilles Lambert, *Caravaggio 1571–1610*, Cologne et al., 2000, and John T. Spike, *Caravaggio*, New York 2001 – a lavishly illustrated volume containing the results of more than twenty years of research.

The vicissitudes of Caravaggio's life on the margin of society, always on the run from the long arm of the law, has stirred the imagination of **novelists and film directors.** Entertaining reads include Iain Pears's *Death and Restoration*, Berkley 2000, Atle Naess, *Doubting Thomas*, London 2000, and Peter Robb, *M – The Man who became Caravaggio*, London 2000. There have also been two biopics on Caravaggio: Umberto Barbaro and the art historian Roberto Longhi's Italian film of 1948, and Derek Jarman's *Caravaggio* of 1986.

Caravaggio: Portraits and Self-Portraits

Unlike most masters of the Baroque, Caravaggio left behind neither written documents nor full-scale self-portraits which could give an insight into the artist as a private person or into his work. Small self-portraits have therefore constantly been sought – and ultimately found – in the paintings themselves. Caravaggio occasionally added his own features to mythological and Biblical characters or secondary figures in

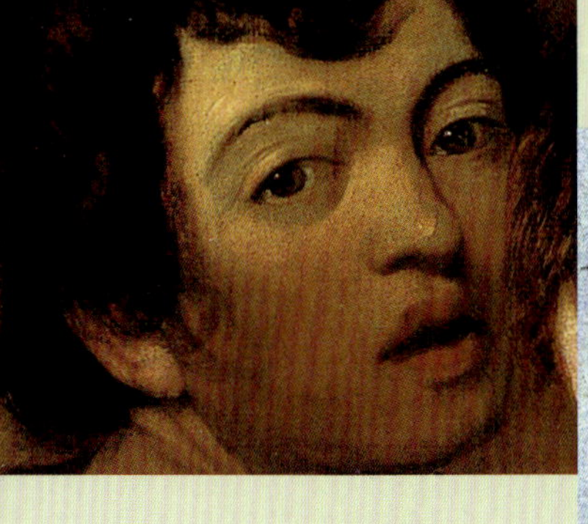

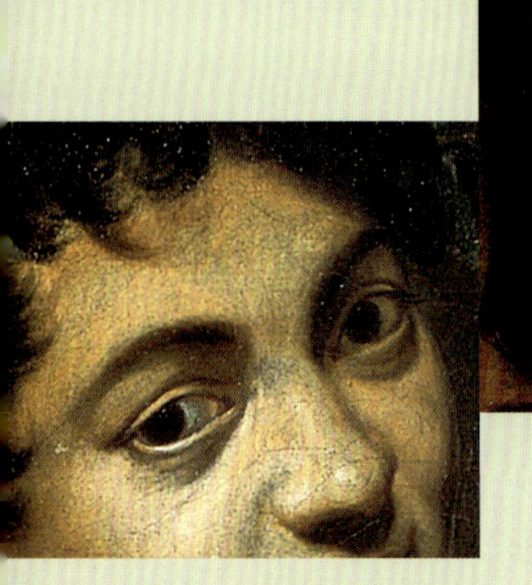

the history paintings, leaving posterity only with half-disguised self-representations to analyse. His external appearance was described to us by his fellow painter Baglione who wrote spitefully that he was "of small stature with an ugly face." Bellori on the other hand simply observed that "he had a swarthy complexion and dark eyes, eyebrows and hair."

The first painting accepted as a self-portrait is *Bacchus* (1593/94), produced shortly after Caravaggio's arrival in Rome. The artist presents himself as a sick god of wine, gazing directly out of the portrait with ivory-garlanded head and slightly open mouth. But, as in other pictures of Bacchus, he looks more like a young man in fancy dress than a god, albeit with an unhealthy olive flush to the skin and pale lips.

Another figure considered to be self-portrait is the horn-player in *The Musicians*, with his pale, beardless face and dark hair. With a slightly open, sensual mouth and raised hand, he seems caught in mid-movement, as if by surprise. He is the only one of the four youths in the picture to be in direct eye contact with the viewer.

The only actual portrait of Caravaggio is by his contemporary Ottavio Leoni and shows a middle-aged man with serious features and large eyes beneath powerful black eyebrows, with a bushy walrus moustache and Egyptian goatee, plus a mop of dark, rather curly hair. The sitter seems to have just turned to look at the viewer. This portrait provided the key to identifying self-portraits in other paintings, although it has never stopped critics arguing as to their authenticity.

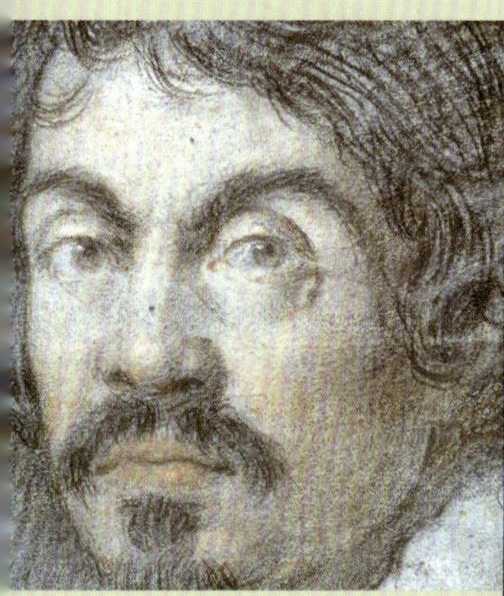

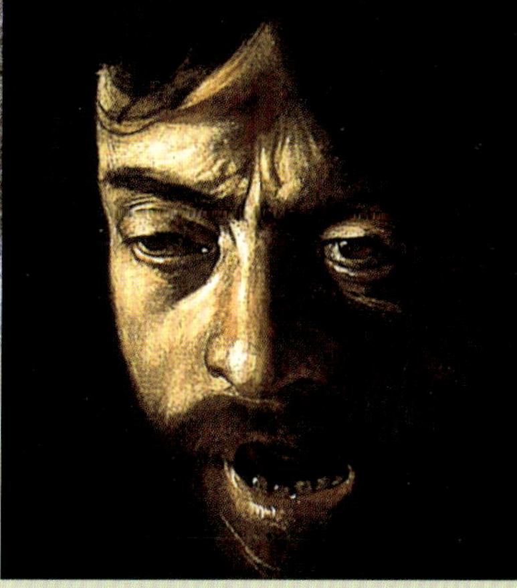

In *David with the Head of Goliath* Caravaggio has lent his own features to the horribly distorted face of the severed head. This portrait is seen as a homage to Michelangelo, who in the *Last Judgment* in the Sistine Chapel likewise gave the flayed apostle Bartholomew his own facial features. But whereas Michelangelo put his face on the skin of a saint, Caravaggio identified himself with one of the damned.

alla prima (Ital. 'straight away'): Technique where a painting is painted directly on to the canvas without preparatory studies or drawings. This technique was common in the sixteenth century, but was most thoroughly exploited by the Impressionists in the nineteenth century.

allegory: A visual illustration of abstract concepts rather like a simile. Common subjects were the virtues (Love, Faith and Hope) or vices (Envy etc.). It is mostly to be found as a personification, i.e. a figure provided with the attributes stands for the abstract concept.

attribute (Lat. *attributum*): An object or entity in a work of art associated with a person for identification purposes; also a symbol caracterising a person, usually based on some characteristic or event in their lives. Over time, in mythology and ecclesiastical or secular history, certain historical figures became inextricably linked to an object thus enabling the viewer to recognise the identity of each figure.

chiaroscuro: (Ital.) Term for the artistic use of light and shadow in a painting, drawing or etching. Its invention is generally associated with the career of Leonardo da Vinci and the rise of oil painting that reached a climax with the work of Caravaggio in Italy, Rembrandt in Holland and Georges de la Tour in Lorraine. This almost imperceptible gradation of light and dark was subsequently applied by Baroque painters all over Europe.

genre painting: A type of painting where the subject matter consists of scenes and events in everyday life. The figures are not portraits and are depicted carrying out a variety of activities such as eating, drinking, cooking or other domestic or daily chores.

history painting: A genre of painting where Biblical, mythological and historical scenes dicatated the content.

In the hierarchy of genres propounded by art academies, history painting was considered the highest, ahead of portraiture, genre painting, animal scenes, landscape painting and still lifes.

naturalism: A style of painting and literary narrative in which it is endeavoured to reproduce empirically tangible reality as faithfully and accurately as possible. A trend towards the direct imitation of nature in painting emerged around 1600 at the same time as more idealising styles, which aimed at 'improving' nature through art.

pictorial plane: The spatial structure of a painting is perceived in terms of pictorial planes – foreground, middle ground and background. The foreground coincides with the surface of the picture, while the planes further back are suggested by paler colours or tinges of blue (air perspective) and the perspective treatment of objects and people. Spatiality can also be suggested by overlapping.

repoussoir (Fr. 'push back'): Figures or objects in the foreground in a painting that steer the eye into the depths of the scene and thus increase the illusion of space and focus the eye on the main event of the picture in the background.

still life (Fr. *nature morte*, Ital. *natura morta*): Genre of painting in which plants (flowers and fruit), objects (books, vessels) and dead animals (especially game) are depicted, arranged into an artistic scene. The fashion for still lifes was particularly strong in Dutch seventeenth-century painting.

tempera: an emulsion used as a medium for a pigment, traditionally, but not exclusively, made with eggs. It dries extremely quickly and was widely used by Italian painters in the fourteenth and fifteenth centuries for fresco painting.

Front cover and inside front flap: **Victorious Cupid** (detail), see p. 42
Back cover: **Madonna dei Pellegrini** (detail), see p. 41

Photographic credits: pp. cover, inside front flap, 11 top, 21, 23, 34, 37, 42, 58, 61 top: Artothek, Weilheim _ pp. 5, 8, 10, 12, 22, 26, 27, 28, 35, 36, 38 right, 40, 41, 47, 48, 52, 53, 54, 55, 61, back cover: © Scala 2005 _ p. 6: S. Fedele, Milan _ p. 7: Brera, Milan _ p. 11 bottom: Palazzo Colonna, Rome _ p. 13 top: Museo di Capodimonte, Naples _ p. 13 bottom: Wadsworth Atheneum, Hartford _ p. 14: Kimbell.Art Museum, Fort Worth _ pp. 19, 20: Metropolitan Museum of Art, New York _ p. 20 top: John and Mable Ringling Museum of Art, Sarasota _ pp. 24, 25, 39, 51: The Bridgeman Art Library _ p. 25: Galleria Doria Pamphilj, Rome _ p. 33: Biblioteca Marucelliana, Florence _ p. 49: Kunsthistorisches Museum, Vienna _ p. 50: Musée des Beaux-Arts, Rouen _ p. 57: Banca Commerciale Italiana, Naples

The Library of Congress Cataloguing-in-Publication data is available; British Library Cataloguing-in-Publication Data: a catalogue record for this book is available from the British Library; Deutsche Bibliothek holds a record of this publication in the Deutsche Nationalbibliografie; detailed bibliographical data can be found under: http://dnb.ddb.de

Prestel Verlag
Königinstrasse 9, 80539 Munich
Tel. +49 (89) 38 17 09-0; Fax +49 (89) 38 17 09-35

Prestel Publishing Ltd.
4 Bloomsbury Place, London WC1A 2QA
Tel. +44 (020) 7323-5004; Fax +44 (020) 7636-8004

Prestel Publishing
900 Broadway, Suite 603, New York, NY 10003
Tel. +1 (212) 995-2720; Fax +1 (212) 995-2733

www.prestel.com

Series concept: **Victoria Salley**
Graphics: **www.lupe.it**, Bolzano, Italy
Translated from the German by **Paul Aston**
Copy-edited by **Christopher Wynne**
Designed and typeset by **zwischenschritt** and **a.visus**, Munich
Originations by **ReproLine mediateam**, Munich
Printed and bound by **Gotteswinter**, Munich

Printed in Germany on acid-free paper
ISBN 3-7913-3321-6